STOP THE SCHOOL BUS

STOP THE SCHOOL BUS

GETTING EDUCATION REFORM BACK ON TRACK

GERALD N. TIROZZI

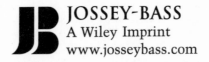

JOSSEY-BASS
A Wiley Imprint
www.josseybass.com

Published by Jossey-Bass
A Wiley Imprint
One Montgomery Street, Suite 1200, San Francisco, CA 94104-4594—
www.josseybass.com

Jossey-Bass books and products are available through most bookstores. To contact Jossey-Bass directly call our Customer Care Department within the U.S. at 800-956-7739, outside the U.S. at 317-572-3986, or fax 317-572-4002.

Wiley publishes in a variety of print and electronic formats and by print-on-demand. Some material included with standard print versions of this book may not be included in e-books or in print-on-demand. If this book refers to media such as a CD or DVD that is not included in the version you purchased, you may download this material at http://booksupport.wiley.com. For more information about Wiley products, visit www.wiley.com.

Library of Congress Cataloging-in-Publication Data has been applied for and is on file with the Library of Congress.
ISBN 978-1-118-25662-6 (cloth),   ISBN 978-1-118-28306-6 (ebk),
ISBN 978-1-118-28352-3 (ebk),   ISBN 978-1-118-28609-8 (ebk)

Printed in the United States of America
FIRST EDITION
HB Printing   10   9   8   7   6   5   4   3   2   1

CONTENTS

About the Author   vii

About NASSP   ix

Acknowledgments   xi

Introduction   xvii

**Part One   America's Teachers: "We Are the
             Heroes We Have Been Waiting for"**

1 To Teach or Not to Teach? How
      Reforms Are Killing the Profession   3

2 Alternate Certification Is the Answer:
      But What Was the Question?   15

3 Performance Pay for Teachers:
      Separating Myth from Reality   37

4 Teacher Bashing: To What End?   51

5 Getting Teacher Reform Back on Track   59

**Part Two   Charter Schools: Helping or
             Hurting School Reform?**

6 Charter Schools: A Dream Denied   91

7 The Equity Problem   103

8 Charter Schools: Innovative *and* Effective?   113

9 Getting Charter Schools Back on Track   121

Part Three   International Comparisons: How They Should and Shouldn't Drive Reform

10 "Oh, to Be in Finland!" A New Look at the Programme for International Student Assessment   133

11 A Trip Down Memory Lane   149

12 Getting International Comparisons Back on Track   157

Part Four   The Federal Role in School Reform: Problems and Solutions

13 Federal School Reform Initiatives: What Happened to Local Control?   165

14 Race to the Top and School Improvement Grants: Helping Schools or Holding Them Hostage?   183

15 Getting the Federal Role Back on Track   195

Conclusion   231

Endnotes   235

Index   251

ABOUT THE AUTHOR

GERALD N. TIROZZI, PH.D., has worked in the field of education for more than 40 years. Most recently he served as Executive Director of the National Association of Secondary School Principals (NASSP), the preeminent organization and the national voice for middle level and high school principals, assistant principals, and aspiring school leaders.

Prior to joining NASSP in March 1999, Dr. Tirozzi held a variety of positions in the field of education including: Assistant Secretary of Elementary and Secondary Education at the U.S. Department of Education (1996–1999); Professor of Educational Leadership at the University of Connecticut (1993–1995); President of Wheelock College (1991–1993); Commissioner of Education in Connecticut (1983–1991); and Superintendent of New Haven (CT) Public Schools (1977–1983). Early in his career, Tirozzi also served as a science teacher, guidance counselor, assistant principal, and principal.

A nationally recognized leader in education reform, Dr. Tirozzi has served on a number of national educational advisory boards, task forces, and professional organizations. Some of these include the: National Board for Professional Teaching Standards (NBPTS), Educational Testing Service

(ETS), Educational Research Service, Evans Newton Incorporated, the Learning First Alliance, Pearson Education National Policy Board, the *USA Today* Education Advisory Panel, and the U.S. Department of State's Overseas Schools Advisory Council.

Dr. Tirozzi's public service and leadership have been recognized by a number of state and national organizations. Some of these include: the Ellis Island Medal of Honor, the Horace Mann League, the U.S. Department of Education, Michigan State University, the U.S. Congress and the Connecticut Legislature.

ABOUT NASSP

The **NATIONAL ASSOCIATION OF SECONDARY SCHOOL PRINCIPALS** promotes excellence in middle level and high school leadership through research-based professional development, resources, and advocacy so that every student can be prepared for postsecondary learning opportunities and be workforce ready.

In existence since 1916, NASSP is the preeminent organization of and national voice for middle level and high school principals, assistant principals, and aspiring school leaders from across the United States and more than 45 countries around the world. The mission of NASSP is to promote excellence in school leadership.

SCHOOL LEADERS

NASSP provides our members with the professional research-based and peer-tested resources, and practical tools and materials they need to serve as visionary school leaders.

Through our award winning publications, professional development opportunities, ready access to relevant research, and persistence in advocating on behalf of school leaders, we help to advance middle level and high school education by:

- Promoting high professional standards
- Focusing attention on school leaders' challenges
- Providing a "national voice" for school leaders
- Building public confidence in education
- Strengthening the role of the principal as instructional leader
- Publicizing the issues and interests of our members in the news media
- Student Leaders

NASSP also promotes the intellectual growth, academic achievement, character and leadership development, and physical well-being of youth. NASSP is proud to have founded and to administer the following student leadership programs:

- National Honor Society and National Junior Honor Society
- National Association of Student Councils
- National Elementary Honor Society

ACKNOWLEDGMENTS

In writing this book, I was fortunate to be in a position to build on my fifty-plus years of experience in public education. During this lengthy period of time, I crossed paths with many outstanding educators, enlightened school board members, committed parents, impressive students, and informed legislative leaders. Each of these groups played an important role in influencing my thinking on school reform. Their collective wisdom provided me with a greater understanding of, and appreciation for, the urgent need to improve public education in a comprehensive and sustainable way—rather than rushing to judgment in formulating school improvement strategies.

This book not only reflects my thinking on school reform but also echoes the "voices" of significant others in the continuing struggle to promote equality and excellence for all students.

I thank the New Haven, Connecticut, public school district for giving me the opportunity to work there for twenty years, initially as a teacher and principal, and eventually as superintendent of schools for six years. It was in New Haven where I first came to understand the countless and complex issues and realities that have an impact on urban schools. This experience awakened me to the need for a multifaceted approach to school improvement, one that transcends the schoolhouse and reaches into the broader community.

I was truly blessed during my tenure as Connecticut's commissioner of education to work with an outstanding group of educators whose skill sets and commitment to viable school reform elevated Connecticut's standing as a national leader in school improvement. Much of this book is gleaned from my daily interactions with this group of dedicated individuals—and from the major accomplishments we achieved—over an exciting and rewarding eight-year period. In particular, I extend my deepest appreciation to Ted Sergi, Pat Forgione, Betty Sternberg, Ray Peschione, Mitch Chester, Doug Rindone, and Steve Leinwand for their support and vision during my tenure. This group of individuals provided me with a leadership team of unparalleled visionaries in school reform. I have watched proudly over the years as these individuals have advanced their careers as chief state school officers, school superintendents, university professors, and "think tank" participants.

I would be remiss if I did not acknowledge former U.S. secretary of education Richard Riley, for whom I had the honor and privilege of working during my tenure as the U.S. Department of Education's assistant secretary of elementary and secondary education. Secretary Riley was both a mentor and a role model to me in his never-ending quest to promote equal educational opportunity for all of our nation's students. His unwavering resolve served to reinforce my own sense of commitment, and parts of this book represent the knowledge I gained from working for this amazing man.

Also, I express my thanks to Marian Herme and Wayne Schmidt, professors at Grand Canyon University in Arizona, for collaborating with me on a published paper on pay for performance for teachers. This paper provided added insight into this timely topic, which is highlighted in this book.

It is important that I highlight the twelve years I spent as the executive director of the National Association of Secondary Principals (NASSP). In this position, I had the opportunity to work with an outstanding staff as well as enlightened and dedicated NASSP board members. My experience at NASSP gave me an even greater appreciation for the essential role of the school principal in school reform—and the need to transform this role into one of instructional leadership. I need to acknowledge several members of the staff who displayed a strong commitment to meaningful school reform through their various programs and initiatives, and whose efforts influenced my thinking on school improvement strategies. Initially, I express my gratitude to Lenor Hersey, my deputy, whose stewardship of the daily management of NASSP afforded me the time necessary to be highly visible in the school reform arena. I also thank Dick Flanary, director of program services, and members of his staff; Patty Kinney; John Nori; Pete Reed; Judith Richardson; and Mel Riddle. I also express my gratitude to Bob Farrace, NASSP director of publications, for continually encouraging me to write about timely and pertinent school reform topics and issues. I also need to send kudos to Beverly Coney, my longtime executive assistant, for "taking care of business," which in turn gave me the opportunity to be "on the road" and engaged as a recognized spokesperson in addressing misguided and ill-informed school reform policies. My tenure at NASSP represented my last full-time leadership position in promoting the goals of comprehensive and sustainable school improvement, and certain parts of the book addressing teacher and principal reform had their genesis during this period.

I also need to acknowledge those individuals whose work intensified my unwavering commitment to preschool and early childhood education, as well as a deep respect for the important role of a school's community. These individuals have had a profound influence on my resolve: Edmund Zigler, the "father" of Head Start; Matia Finn-Stevenson, a founder, along with Zigler, of the "School of the 21st Century" model, and James Comer, founder of the nationally recognized "Comer Model" of school improvement. I believe that these areas, prominently referenced in the book, should represent the foundational underpinnings of all school reform initiatives.

I also wish to acknowledge the ongoing support of Margie McAneny, senior editor at Jossey-Bass, who provided me with much-appreciated assistance and guidance throughout the process. Her insightful recommendations represented valued contributions as I continually worked to improve the original manuscript. Also, her ongoing words of encouragement played a major role in my seeing the publication of the book through to fruition. In addition, I extend my gratitude to Francie Jones, copy editor at Jossey-Bass, for providing her editorial skills in improving the final manuscript.

Finally, I am deeply grateful to my wife, Sharman Mc-Kinnon, for her continuing support and understanding while I was consumed with writing this book. She never complained when I spent countless hours dedicated to research and writing—which took away from family activities and vacation time. I thank her for being at my side throughout the process, for her continuing words of inspiration, and for her constant faith in my abilities.

INTRODUCTION

The title of this book, *Stop the School Bus*, is a metaphor depicting what is, in my view, the ill-advised route of school reform in recent years. With this title I aim to send the strong message that it is better to get off the bus than to continue on a misdirected school reform journey—one that fails to address the needs of students and educators; recommends strategies and programs that often have no research base; doesn't always live up to promises; places an onerous burden on schools and educators; and in some cases uses a "smoke and mirrors" depiction of success.

Consider the adults on the bus. Jim Collins, in his book *Good to Great*,[1] stresses the importance—in any organization—of having the right people on board. The majority of those driving many of today's school reform efforts have never worked in or even attended a public school; a significant number are foundation and corporate leaders whose primary goal is, arguably, to privatize public education; and of course there are the so-called education policy "gurus." Furthermore, these "reformers" driving the bus put forth views based on a reality that is far removed from what takes place in public school classrooms daily.

What is frustrating here is that no other profession would allow similar "outsiders" to have such a marked influence on the policies and initiatives that drive and influence it. It would be unthinkable to envision other professions (medicine, dentistry, law, architecture, engineering, and so on) allowing outside individuals to diagnose their problems and to apply the remedies.

There is something truly wrong with the fact that the education profession allows these "external influences" to continue to dictate the reform agenda for public schools. It is time for educators to take over the "driver's seat." They need to use their experience and knowledge base to redirect school reform efforts toward viable and sustained school improvement strategies.

My primary goal in writing this was to sound a wake-up call for educators to take back their profession. An additional purpose is to help clarify for federal officials, state and local legislators, and policymakers the myriad issues and onerous concerns embodied in the present array of school reform initiatives. Above all, I hope this book provides all of these audiences with a new *vision* for school improvement. This vision is embedded in the comprehensive recommendations provided at the end of each part. These recommendations, if considered and implemented, can move school reform on a new course—and one that can be traveled by all constituent groups on a cooperative and supportive pathway.

The book is divided into four parts, each representing a timely and major area of school improvement. Part One analyzes today's teacher reform efforts, Part Two reviews the impact of charter schools, Part Three assesses the achievement comparisons of the United States with such other countries as Finland and Singapore, and Part Four examines the role of the federal government in education. The last chapter in each part examines relevant possible reform strategies, the majority of which are intended to address the misguided and ill-advised existing reform strategies cited within that part.

There will be those who disagree with the opinions, findings, and recommendations provided in this book. However, as one who has lived the experience of public education at all levels over the past fifty years, I stand behind this book as an informed analysis of current school reform initiatives. During my career I have worked as a classroom teacher, principal, school superintendent, college president, and university professor, and as the U.S. assistant secretary of education. Most recently I retired as executive director of the National Association of Secondary School Principals. I hope, therefore, that my review of the school reform initiatives of recent years—and my reform vision for the future—will have clout with those who toil daily in the vineyard of public education, and will provide a new vision for school improvement.

In addition, my hope is that those who are driving school improvement efforts will give greater standing to the issues and concerns raised, and to this new vision for reform—respecting that these are presented from the perspective of an experienced education practitioner.

The yellow school bus is a symbol of American public education, which must soon embark on a new route. A successful new route will require a new set of drivers who are prepared to "take the road less traveled," accompanied by a multitude of riders who are committed to meaningful systemic and sustainable school improvement practices. I hope everyone is ready to board!

STOP THE SCHOOL BUS

Part One

AMERICA'S TEACHERS: "WE ARE THE HEROES WE HAVE BEEN WAITING FOR"

Chapter One

TO TEACH OR NOT TO TEACH? HOW REFORMS ARE KILLING THE PROFESSION

John Gesmonde, an attorney in Connecticut with extensive experience in education litigation, arbitration, and mediation, has used Michael Jackson's iconic "moonwalk" to portray the illusionary onward movement—while sliding backward—of the education reform efforts driven by federal, state, and local officials.[1] The reality is that many of the legislative acts and school board policies under consideration, or enacted, represent giant steps backward in recruiting and retaining a highly competent teacher workforce.

To teach or not to teach? This is an important question on the minds of those who are considering a career in teaching—and a timely topic in the continuing national discourse on improving our nation's schools. It represents a seminal issue in regard to not only the skills and abilities of the individuals who will teach America's children but also what level of long-term commitment these individuals will have to the teaching profession. Regrettably, the recent ill-advised and morale-shattering teacher reform strategies of state legislators, governors, and municipal leaders—partly fueled by their obsession with "racing to the money"—have become pursuits fueled by the misguided mandates of the Race to the Top and School Improvement Grants initiatives. This obsession has apparently caused them not to consider the impact of their decisions on prospective teachers considering whether or not to enter the profession—or to stay in the profession.

Consider recent policy developments in many school districts that have resulted in overturning collective bargaining rights; depleting health benefits; dismantling tenure; promoting merit pay; and removing seniority and job security. Taken collectively, these changes have largely served as disincentives for individuals to enter the teaching profession or to remain in teaching. They also represent a blatant disregard for the hard work and dedication of our nation's teaching force. Are there incompetent teachers? Yes. Should such teachers be replaced? Of course. Do tenure and seniority present a problem? Without question. But addressing these problems as systemic rather than as individual personnel issues represents a frontal attack on the vast universe of teachers who daily perform one of our nation's greatest services—teaching our students.

Now also consider the negative impact of the recent wave of legislative actions and other school district edicts to take away from teachers the rights and benefits that have long been major components of their profession, and that they have fought long and hard to retain. Finally, consider the realistic impact of the isolated world within which a teacher works, generally confined to the walls of her or his classroom and void of contact with other adults during the school day.

Would You Take This Job? What an Honest Marketing Tool to Teachers Would Look Like

To help readers fully appreciate the impact of escalating legislative actions, school board policies, and timeworn realities on the teaching profession, I have developed a recruitment tool that in my opinion reflects these considerations. Critics may suggest that the picture I paint of the conditions teachers face is overkill. They may also take exception to my characterization of the isolated lifestyle of a classroom teacher. As a rejoinder, let me say that it is my firm conviction that all of the conditions I cite represent a "real and present danger," and a potentially catastrophic future, for school districts in their recruitment of a teaching force. This danger is a direct result of the policies and legislation that unappreciative and inadequately informed federal officials, state legislators, and local school boards have implemented, or have under consideration. I predict that their unwise and rash manifestations have the potential to change forever the landscape of a proud profession.

Why Choose Teaching as a Career? Important Facts (Or, an Honest Recruitment Tool)

1. *You will receive drastically reduced health benefits compared to what teachers have traditionally received, the cost of which will now be your responsibility,* even though your salary will remain well below those of other professions requiring similar qualifications.

(Continued)

2. *You will continue to receive a substandard salary compared to those of other professions.* On average, the national starting salary of new teachers is approximately $39,000. The region of the country where you plan to teach will determine your specific starting salary. Keep in mind that many states have starting salaries that are very low, in the mid- to high-$20,000 range. It is expected that these much lower salaries will not dissuade you from making a career decision to enter the profession. After all, it appears to be the general consensus of the naysayers of the profession—those individuals who have lost faith in public education and its teachers—that teachers, unlike other professionals, seemingly do not need financial stability in their lives, and that they teach for the love of what they do!

3. *You will be expected to work long hours every day, and often on weekends*—contrary to what those individuals far removed from classroom realities believe or understand to be a teacher's work schedule. Your extended days will be a result of what is expected of classroom teachers, such as

   - Class and individual student lesson planning
   - Correcting student papers and grading student performance
   - Participating in professional development activities to enhance your area of expertise
   - Continual online communication and face-to-face conferences with students and parents
   - Ongoing consultation with other teachers and professional staff

- Attending planning and placement sessions for students with special needs
- Completing the never-ending paperwork requirements imposed by administrators

Unfortunately, the majority of these responsibilities—unlike in other professions in which sufficient time is provided during the regular workday—must take place outside of traditional work hours, in that teachers are not allocated time in their school day to accomplish these countless and complex responsibilities.

4. *You will have little, if any, free time during the traditional 8:00 a.m. to 3:30 p.m. school day*, a condition that is especially true for elementary and self-contained classroom teachers. You will not, in effect, have time for consulting with other teachers in the building, taking an occasional ten-minute respite from your classroom responsibilities, enjoying a coffee break with colleagues, or contacting parents—and unless you really learn to control your urinary tract, you may not have time to pee! Of course, if this latter problem persists, legislators, again displaying their infinite wisdom, may very well enact legislation to ensure the necessary funding to provide interested teachers with catheters (kidding, of course!).

Keep in mind that some individuals continually articulate that teachers have a "cushy" work schedule. As they make such ridiculous pronouncements, they will continue to have opportunities throughout their

(Continued)

workday for numerous coffee breaks; intervals of relaxation; regular interaction with their colleagues; and a lengthy lunch period—away from the work environment, often at a local restaurant. Amazingly, they may also use a lavatory whenever their bodily needs arise! But alas, they still lament that they do not have the "cushy" lifestyle of a teacher.

5. *You will have to learn to eat your lunch within about twenty to thirty minutes, and in many cases you will have to digest your food while in the presence of your students.* Of course, in the vast majority of cases, you will not be allowed leave the school grounds to have your lunch—and meeting family and friends over the lunch hour is a definite no-no.

6. *You must be prepared to have your annual evaluation partially or in some cases almost wholly based on a state test administered once each school year.* Whatever other assessments and learning activities your students engage in on the remaining 179 days of the school year are not likely to carry the same weight with evaluators as this single state test. Also, consider putting aside any interest you may have in teaching subjects that may instill in students an interest in and excitement for learning, such as the arts, the humanities, physical education, and others. Regrettably, you will probably receive zero evaluation credit for your efforts or accomplishments in these subject areas.

   You should be aware that your annual evaluation results might improve dramatically, simply by your seeking a job opportunity in a state that has lower proficiency standards for students. Conversely, if you receive a satisfactory evaluation in your state, you should exercise great caution in considering a transfer to a state with higher proficiency standards for students. The ultimate irony is that all states set their own proficiency standards, so an incompetent teacher in one state may be a superstar in another— or vice versa. So much for fairness and logic!

7. *Your annual evaluation may be made publicly available to parents, students, the general public, and the news media.* Such public notice may also include rankings of teachers from best to worst. These rankings will probably not distinguish between teachers working in an affluent neighborhood school and teachers working in a school serving an impoverished community. It is more than likely that the rankings will not take into consideration the number of English language learners in your classroom, nor will they reflect the number of your students with special needs. You may, of course, make a career decision to apply or transfer to a school or district in your state with a high percentage of students from affluent homes, and with fewer students in need of academic assistance. A simple move of this type would almost certainly guarantee that your public image, status, and ranking as a teacher will be dramatically elevated.

8. *You may work in a school system that, based on legislative actions or school board policies, does not protect the*

(*Continued*)

seniority status of teachers. Although you may eventually have several years of experience and receive satisfactory evaluations for those years, your position has the potential to be furloughed or terminated. Without the protection of seniority, a school superintendent may, for personal reasons, summarily decide to dismiss you. Alternatively, such a decision may be initiated by a disgruntled board of education member or a local legislator for highly questionable reasons, including a personal dislike for you as a teacher, unkind feedback from parents, a desire to fill the position with a friend or relative, or political patronage. This type of "dishonesty" in personnel decisions will be exacerbated as seniority in teaching becomes a faint memory.

The fact is that teachers' union contracts were historically written with school boards to ensure that such nefarious personnel practices were minimized, and that teachers' rights were upheld. It now appears that the potential exists for superintendents, school board members, and local legislators to return to the practices exhibited in the "dark days" before seniority. During this period, it was common to see unsubstantiated, ill-advised, and in some cases illegal decisions in the hiring and firing of teachers.

Although there are, without question, senior teachers with poor evaluations who should be terminated, state and local leaders are choosing to illogically place all senior teachers in the same box—instead of committing to addressing seniority problems as individual personnel decisions. In addition, if local administrators had been diligent over the years in their supervision and evaluation responsibilities, ineffective senior teachers would have been identified much earlier. And if these teachers had not improved their practice, they would have been terminated prior to receiving tenure.

9. *You will have to come to grips with the reality that although your career choice to become a teacher represents a noble and grand commitment,* a career in teaching essentially removes you from the financial stability, multiple benefits, social standing, and professional appreciation another career might afford. But always keep in mind that the joy of teaching far exceeds the "superficial rewards" of other well-paid and socially elevated professions!

10. *You need to be ready, as a member of the teaching profession, to accept the blame for all of society's problems,* including the downturn in the economy, the decline in our nation's standing as a world power, and any other circumstance or event for which a scapegoat is not readily available!

You should carefully consider all of the realities of teaching just listed prior to deciding to enter the teaching profession. Although admittedly there are major and troublesome changes and disruptions on the horizon, great teachers always overcome such obstacles and become champions for their enduring commitment to children. I hope you will make the right decision!

A Personal Reflection on the New Realities for Teachers

My representation of the realities facing teachers is not intended to dissuade interested and committed young people from choosing what I consider to be a wonderful, inspiring, and fulfilling career path. However, I feel compelled to bring into clear perspective the effects of many legislative and school board actions and policies that may result in fewer young people entering the profession. I am also confronted with the reality that veteran teachers may decide that they have experienced enough professional adversity and inadequate appreciation—*the end result being that they may decide to move on to other career opportunities.*

As someone who has devoted his life to education, I find it enormously frustrating to observe the various machinations of far-removed legislators and not-very-well-informed school board members that wreak unwarranted and undeserved havoc on teachers. Teachers are professionals who on a daily basis offer their expertise to, and show their love for, our nation's most importance resource—its children. They daily perform magnanimous work—in spite of minimal salaries, a lack of appreciation for their efforts, and a continuing avalanche of disdain from government and corporate leaders. They do not deserve the cascades of reform that threaten to drown them—and to forever change the landscape and environment of the teaching profession.

I can't help but feel anger and resentment toward federal and state legislators, policy gurus, and foundation and corporate leaders who are largely responsible for setting an agenda for teacher reform—many components of which translate into a form of "teacher bashing." They are only serving to remove teachers from decisions and actions that have an impact on their profession and their very livelihood. My anger is intensified by the reality that their actions and the onerous burdens they impose on teachers are taking the "soul" out of teaching—the essence of what teaching is, including creativity, professionalism, inspiration, devotion, commitment, and pride. If they are successful in removing the soul, they will leave behind a hollow teaching force of script-following and uninspired classroom automatons —an outcome that violates the underlying principles of respect and honor for a profession dedicated to educating our nation's children.

In spite of my concerns, I also feel a sense of hope and optimism, engendered by a belief that the issues and concerns I have articulated will capture the attention of those individuals who continue to be naysayers of the teaching profession—who have demonstrated little or no respect for teachers, as evidenced by their ill-advised legislative actions and policies. The publication of this book is intended to cause such an "awakening."

This awakening would ideally cause the "distant reformers" to pause in imposing their will on our nation's teachers. I hope they can truly be brought to understand the negative, demeaning, and demoralizing impact of their ill-founded actions and policies on our nation's teachers. I hope they will step back and repair, modify, and dismantle, in a timely manner, the egregious reform initiatives they have placed in the path of teachers. It can reasonably be projected that if these reforms go unmodified, they may very well result in the demise of a proud profession.

ONE TEACHER'S LAMENT

To give credence to my deep concerns, consider the lament of one experienced and highly regarded teacher. Angela Beeley, a National Board Certified Teacher in California, expresses her views on the frustration and anger of teachers in her 2011 article "Mad as Hell." Her commentary is on target and should be required reading for federal officials, legislators, and school board members who continually display errant behavior in shaping laws and policies that are detrimental to the future of the teaching profession. Beeley writes: "I love my students, but who on earth does the public—which is accepting these political shenanigans—think will choose to become a teacher now? No one in his or her right mind would go into this profession. After seeing teachers beaten up in the media for our society's failings and being portrayed as lazy fat cats, when we are working our butts off having to 'teach' to a test, no student with two brain cells to rub together is going to want to become a teacher."[2]

Beeley also offers, in the same editorial, a challenge to Wisconsin's governor, an architect of some of the most egregious "teacher bashing" legislation in the nation, as well as to others who continually put teachers down: "I challenge anyone—including Wisconsin's governor—who thinks that teaching requires little effort, no summer break or no decent salary, to spend a year in my classroom. Get in there, Governor Walker. You wouldn't last a week."[3]

I suspect there are legions of teachers who share Beeley's frustration and disdain concerning the avalanche of onerous and debilitating teacher reform legislation and policies —and who share her view as to the dismal future of teacher recruitment.

Chapter Two

ALTERNATE CERTIFICATION IS THE ANSWER: BUT WHAT WAS THE QUESTION?

I am often tempted, when engaging in a discussion about the escalating movement to maximize the number of individuals entering teaching through a "back door," to consider having a button made that reads: *If alternate certification is the answer, what the hell was the question?* Many federal, state, and local officials—along with corporate and foundation leaders and policy gurus—often present different pathways to certification as the answer to the question of how to improve schools. They express a point of view that problems associated with closing the achievement gap, staffing "turnaround schools," filling teacher vacancies, and meeting the academic needs of low-income students can be addressed by nontraditionally trained teachers.

I would posit that their answer, which has no research base, represents a "quick fix" to address very complex problems and avoid confronting the important question of how to build and sustain a profession of teachers. This answer fails to take into account the quintessential requirements of a teaching career: being conversant with both the art and science of teaching, understanding how children grow and develop, being cognizant of different learning modalities, and possessing the requisite skill sets to address individual student needs. Conversely, the advocates of alternate routes to teaching seemingly reduce their basic concerns about school reform and teacher engagement to a very simple question: How do we recruit the brightest college graduates to teach in our lowest-performing schools, and with students who have the greatest academic needs? Although this question initially appears to have a laudatory goal, carefully consider other questions that apparently are not on these advocates' radar screen, and whose answers make alternate certification a suspect route to viable school reform:

- How prepared are these "instant teachers" to teach students with the greatest academic needs?
- Is it fair to students with significant academic needs in low-income urban areas to allow "itinerant workers" to temporarily drop in on their lives, simply because these teachers are considered to be "better educated"?
- Is having a strong knowledge base in a particular academic subject area, which represents only one component of a fully prepared teacher's repertoire, sufficient to accomplish the task of teaching students with the greatest academic needs?
- What level of long-term commitment exists for teachers entering though this back door, whose very recruitment is often predicated on a future promise of being better prepared to move into a higher-paying position in busi-

ness, law, or medicine? Alternatively, in how many cases do they plan to use their teaching experience as a "stepping stone" to gain admission to a prestigious graduate school?

- Where are the long-term research and evaluation data that support the successes and accomplishments of alternatively certified teachers when compared to traditionally prepared teachers?

- Is there any other profession that would allow individuals who have taken an alternate route to certification to substitute as professionals in their disciplines? To further expand on this question, would anyone of sound mind consider asking an alternatively certified doctor to perform surgery, dentist to perform a root canal, architect to design a house, or lawyer to defend a lawsuit?

- Do the zealots in favor of expanding alternate certification really believe that anyone with a college or university degree can teach, and are they prepared to have this "anyone" teach their own children?

Clearly those who advocate alternative paths for teachers have to some degree lost respect for the profession—a profession that, for the vast majority of these advocates, provided the educational foundation on which they built their professional and personal lives. I would suggest that this loss of respect not only has no basis but also sends reformers barking up the wrong tree in an effort to fix our schools. Consider one reform effort designed to attract a whole corps of excited and talented new people to the profession: Teach for America (TFA).

Teach for America: Has It Helped Our Schools?

This initiative had its genesis in 1990 when Wendy Kopp wrote her senior thesis at Princeton, in which she developed her idea of recruiting outstanding graduates from elite colleges and universities into a new teacher corps. The main component of the TFA initiative allowed for the new recruits to teach for two years largely in low-income urban schools. The program has grown under Kopp's leadership and has, since 1990, placed approximately thirty-three thousand recruits into teaching positions in high-need schools.

I would be remiss if I did not initially acknowledge Kopp's vision, management skills, and fundraising abilities in bringing her dream for TFA to fruition. In addition, I am impressed by the interest and passion exhibited by college and university graduates—mostly from top-tier schools— to teach in urban and other low-income communities. However, an immediate concern arises, one that is shared by many other educators: that TFA's stated intent is to commit its recruits to only two years as teachers in low-income communities. This reality raises an immediate red flag as to the long-term impact and success of such a short-term commitment to teaching.

Consider, for example, that these "teaching interns," with five weeks of summer training, are then placed in classrooms with students who have the greatest academic needs. Granted, these newly minted "interns" each have a strong academic background and certain subject matter expertise. However, such an academic background does not provide them with the necessary pedagogical tools to diversify instruction; a repertoire of varied curricula; an understanding of how best to teach students with special needs and English language learners; and, most important, a background in, and understanding of, child growth and development. Simply stated, an individual cannot acquire these requisite skills and understandings in a five-week summer crash course.

A broad body of research concludes that it generally takes three to five years to become an effective teacher. A major contributor to this research is Linda Darling-Hammond, a distinguished professor at Stanford University and an internationally known and respected expert and researcher in all aspects of the teaching profession. Darling-Hammond has reported, based on a review of state and district data, that fewer than 20 percent of TFA-ers stay in teaching for more than four years.[1] Many large school districts have also reported significant turnover of TFA teachers within a two- to four-year period. For example, a recent study found that by their fourth year, 85 percent of TFA teachers had left the New York City public schools.[2] An unfortunate outcome of this early exodus is that even if some of the TFA graduates had the potential to become highly effective teachers, the significant majority of them left their teaching position within two to three years—leaving behind remnants of what might have been an exemplary teaching career.

Darling-Hammond's research further concludes that this revolving door of TFA recruits represents an estimated average reoccurring cost to school districts of more than $70,000 per recruit, based on the expenses associated with teacher recruitment, training, and replacement. She concludes that this is "enough to have trained numerous effective career teachers."[3]

Several studies concerning TFA's track record have been conducted over the years. It is interesting to note the degree to which several researchers have reached different conclusions, analyzing the same data sets. It's as though the individuals or organizations interpreting the results were viewing works of art and reflecting the adage, "Beauty is in the eye of the beholder."

With such mixed evaluation data, and with such conflicting views about what the findings mean—along with concerns about the validity of certain studies—it appears that the jury is still out as to what, if any, real difference TFA is making in bolstering student achievement and closing the achievement gap. The bigger issue in reviewing the TFA evaluation data is that even if a case can be made for the program's limited success, the reality is that approximately 80 percent of the individuals who are part of this success story leave their classroom within four years. There is, in effect, no continuity in whatever success is realized, and continued efforts must advance with yet another group of "raw recruits." In this respect, TFA has exhibited no real interest in building a profession. It is seemingly intent on implementing a "drop in, drop out" approach to improving teaching and student achievement, raising serious questions as to what, if any, long-term impact the program will have in addressing the academic needs of at-risk students.

An often-cited concern with TFA, as already mentioned, is that it asks its teacher recruits to commit to only a two-year "teaching career"—essentially conveying an expectation that the recruits will quickly leave teaching and pursue other career opportunities. This point is very evident in TFA's recruiting literature, which makes it explicitly clear that a two-year career in teaching will open opportunities to pursue other more lucrative career options, and will give recruits an advantage when applying to prestigious graduate schools. In fact, some critics have facetiously referred to TFA as "Teach for a Resume" and "Teach for Awhile"! Mark Naison, a professor at Fordham University, has refused for several years to allow TFA to recruit his students because he was taken aback by the audacity of a TFA recruiter who "plaster[ed] the campus" with flyers that read, "Learn how joining TFA can help you gain admission to the Stanford Business School." Naison expands on his concern by expressing his anger at the message of that flyer—that students could "use teaching in high poverty areas as a stepping stone to a career in business." He adds: "It was not only disrespectful of every person who chooses to commit their life to the teaching profession, it advocated using students in high poverty areas as guinea pigs for an experiment in 'resume padding' for ambitious young people."[4]

TFA is sensitive to the complaints that its recruits are not committed to teaching as a career, and the related issue that its recruitment literature openly and aggressively promotes other avenues of career advancement. The organization's response to these issues and concerns is that TFA alumni remain working or studying in the field of education. TFA points out that its alumni stay active by serving on local and state school boards and seeking legislative offices at both the local and state levels. Barbara Miner, who has written an insightful treatise on TFA, rebuts TFA's claim, and points out that TFA's assertion that its alumni remain in education is misleading: "TFA's definition of education is loosely defined to include everything from working with a non-profit advocacy group to getting a graduate degree."[5]

TFA maintains that its alumni play a major role in formulating education policy and exerting political clout in crafting education legislation—which represents a major deviation from the organization's stated purpose. Some individuals, and most certainly TFA leaders, consider engagement in such public service arenas to be a reflection of their continuing commitment to education. Yet there is another point of view to be considered. At what point did the dialogue on the long-term success of TFA's teaching recruits shift to assessing their "afterlife" in public service?

HAS TEACH FOR AMERICA GIVEN UP ON ITS ORIGINAL MISSION?

One can only speculate as to the degree to which the foundations, corporations, and others that have provided substantial financial resources to TFA fully appreciate TFA's willingness to supplant its initial vision. Funders need to realize that this vision has been seriously compromised; what initially began as a commitment to providing teachers for low-income students has turned into a broader social and political agenda. If, in fact, funders have accepted this expanded TFA universe, then perhaps they have little concern that TFA's central role in recruiting teachers has ostensibly become secondary to a larger agenda. In effect, the funders should have a sense of uneasiness that teaching has taken a "back seat" to TFA's desire to establish a national presence through its alumni network—to exercise "political clout."

It seems that TFA is rapidly changing the "rules of engagement" by moving away from the rationale for its very existence—recruiting teachers—to a vision of national civic and political engagement. This change in direction brings into serious question the continuing role of TFA as a viable player in teacher reform.

The irony is that although TFA trumpets its rapidly growing alumni commitment to civic and political engagement, a 2010 study out of Stanford University found that "TFA alumni actually had lower rates of civic engagement than those who had been accepted by TFA but declined, and also had lower rates than those who dropped out before their two years were completed."[6]

TFA has also been widely recognized as having the ability to generate substantial fiscal support for its endeavors. In fact, TFA is considered a fundraising behemoth. Consider that at TFA's annual dinner in 2008 it raised, in one evening, $5.5 million. At the time it was reported that stretch limousines jammed Park Avenue for blocks—a true attestation to TFA's appeal in the corporate and foundation funding world. To further appreciate the funding juggernaut that TFA has become, consider that in 2010 TFA had an annual operating budget of $185 million—with two-thirds coming from private donations and the rest from government sources. It should be obvious that the "message" of TFA is being heard and supported at the highest economic levels of our society.

There has developed, over the years, a sense among educators that TFA has had a disturbing merging of views with its major funding sources, possibly at the expense of its own original core values. As Miner concludes, "TFA has no public criticism of pro-market reforms such as privatization and for-profit charters. Nor does it ask hard questions about the relations between the achievement gap and problems of segregation, poverty and an unemployment rate among African American men that hovers around 50% in some urban communities."[7]

In the same treatise, Miner further advances her concerns about the degree to which TFA has formed intensive relationships with groups and organizations that have not historically been supporters of public education. Miner points out that several of these groups and organizations are committed to promoting privatization of public schools. She brings to the reader's attention the cogent observations of Wendy Puriefoy, president of the Public Education Network, an association focused on public school reform in low-income communities. Puriefoy, who herself previously served as a member of the TFA board of directors, noted that in providing her analysis she had chosen her words carefully because it was "going to sound harsh."[8] Puriefoy states, "The very same people who promoted economic deregulation are influential supporters of organizations such as Teach for America. They want to sidestep the professional teachers, unions and schools of education, 'and let loose the forces of the markets.'" Puriefoy adds, "The marketplace of education is a big market. There is a lot of money to be made."[9]

Education blogger George Wood adds his own frustration in regard to the escalating push by outside funders to promote market-driven reform strategies, including TFA: "I . . . find it interesting that some of the most powerful

pushers of these ideas are the so-called titans of Wall St.—
the Broad Foundation, Bill Gates of late, and Democrats for
Education Reform (a bunch of well-funded capitalists)." His
quote reinforces the concern that "outside money" is driving
reform—and the reality is that TFA is one of the largest
beneficiaries of such support. Wood concludes with a sar-
castic jab: "Hey, private capital did such a great job with the
economy (and oil wells), why not turn over public schools
to them?"[10]

Indeed it would appear that TFA, in its alleged commitment to recruiting teachers for high-poverty public
schools, has become a veritable "money machine." This is at
the expense of getting much too close to many of the same
individuals who seek to remove the word *public* from our
nation's system of education. To further expand on this
reality, consider two of the major donors to TFA.

The *Wallace Family Foundation* has, based on the
philanthropic beliefs of Wal-Mart founder Sam Walton,
committed over $9 million to TFA—making it TFA's largest
contributor. It is important to note that within the world of
education foundations, Walton is synonymous with privatization and the promotion of vouchers for attending private
schools.

The *Doris and Donald Fisher Fund* has been listed as
giving $2.5 million to TFA. The late Donald Fisher founded
the Gap stores; he made headlines in San Francisco for his
conservative Republican politics and for his various deregulation and privatization plans—including a pledge of $25
million in the late 1990s to expand the for-profit Edison
Schools of California.[11]

CAN PROGRAMS LIKE TFA HELP LOW-PERFORMING STUDENTS?

The most frequent criticism of TFA is probably that the program promotes a teacher intervention reform strategy built on the premise that teaching is best learned in the classroom and doesn't require extensive preparation, in-depth training, and comprehensive study. The criticism builds when it is considered that TFA's minimally trained recruits are then placed in the classrooms of the students with the greatest academic needs, which are located in the nation's poorest communities. Rather than viewing TFA as a turn-around reform strategy, it may be better to characterize it as a "backward" strategy. The reality is that low-performing schools and their students need the best teachers, with proven records of accomplishment, to promote students' educational advancement. What these schools and their students do not need is an invasion of newly minted rookies who, although well intentioned, lack the requisite skill sets and training to meet the needs of students with significant academic needs.

Arthur Levine, former president of Teachers College at Columbia University, has shared his views on TFA: "For inner-city kids, it's a huge disadvantage to have a teacher who doesn't know how to teach. And if the teacher rapidly improves they just as rapidly quit." Such turnover, Levine concludes, "ensures a continuous array of rookies."[12] The problem of having a high concentration of first-year and inexperienced teachers in low-income communities—a problem to which TFA is a contributor—is consistent across the country, and is most pronounced in urban areas. This recurring trend exists even though there is a wide body of research suggesting that teachers with less experience tend to be less effective, especially in their first two years. This research further brings into question TFA's continuing resolve to have its recruits commit to only two years of teaching.

To further expand on this troubling reality of teacher turnover, consider that in 2009 the *Washington Post* conducted a study of school districts in its region and found that the region's poorest schools were twice as likely to have a new or second-year teacher as those in the wealthiest communities. It can reasonably be predicted that similar studies in other large metropolitan areas would have similar findings. This type of inequality in the distribution of teachers between poor and rich communities has relevance for any discussion of to TFA. Consider that TFA is an annual contributor to a "revolving door" approach to staffing our nation's lowest-performing schools. Consider the fairness and equity for disadvantaged students, who will conceivably spend years in classrooms with "raw recruits." Consider that the majority of these recruits will, within two to three years in the classroom, leave to be replaced by yet another group of similar recruits. As Miner asks, "Is TFA aggravating a problem that it claims to be solving?"[13]

If, as a nation, we are committed to addressing the academic needs of disadvantaged students and closing the achievement gap, then we will need teachers who are committed for the long haul. Such an effort will require a teaching force ready to make an extensive time commitment, extend their perseverance and dedication, and acknowledge the importance for students of having continuity in their classrooms. Meaningful school reform necessitates a marathon run for those teachers who are unwavering in their resolve to enhance student learning and promote greater excellence and equity for all students. Unfortunately, as Barnett Berry, head of the Center for Teaching Quality, points out, "TFA gets its recruits ready for a sprint, not a 10 K or a marathon."[14] To this point I would add: "'Sprinters' need not apply!"

A CONUNDRUM FOR TEACHERS: ALTERNATE CERTIFICATION FOR PRINCIPALS

The rush to alternate certification has also allowed several states to dramatically change the entry requirements for new principals. These changes send a message that basically anyone with a bachelor's or master's degree—with some level of management experience, generally outside of education— even if they lack any teaching experience, can become an "instant" principal. Following are summaries of examples of four states and their disjointed approach to principal "preparation," which have been taken directly from a website[15] highlighting state-initiated alternate routes to principal certification. It is important to point out here that alternate certification regulations change in states on a regular basis. However, the key observation to take away from these four examples, whether or not they have been modified since the information was posted on the website, is that they represent illustrations of ill-advised state practices in principal recruitment:

- *Utah*—"However, for administrative candidates, exceptions can be made for exceptional professional experience, exceptional education accomplishments, or other note-worthy experiences or circumstances."[16]

Note: This alternate route basically opens the door wide for just about anyone being tasked as a school principal. Consider the vague and illogical prerequisites cited, especially the reference to "note-worthy experiences or circumstances." Who makes the determination, and using what criteria, to define "note-worthy"? Such dizzying logic completely misses the core requirements necessary to function as a school principal—and more importantly to provide instructional leadership. There is no reference to teaching experience, and yet even without such direct contact with teaching and learning, candidates are expected to provide leadership, understanding, and credibility in regard to curriculum development and instructional processes. What were the crafters of this alternate certification route thinking?

- *New Hampshire*—"Alternative paths to certification are available for administrator candidates demonstrating required competencies and experiences." [17]

  Note: It really is difficult to comprehend what is implied by "demonstrating required competencies and experiences" for individuals who presumably are not in education leadership positions. It would seem logical to assume that if they possessed the requisite skills to be a principal, they would not have to enter through a "back door." A principal's role is very specific, and although it is understood that there are other leadership positions in education—such as athletic directors, department heads, guidance counselors, and so on—

none of these positions requires the preparation and training needed to immediately function as a school principal. It is really a stretch if the alternate route is also available to someone functioning as a manager in some other work environment—expecting that he/she can simply transfer into the principal's role.

- *Massachusetts*—"The commissioner may exempt a district for any one school year from the requirement to employ personnel licensed or certified upon request of a superintendent and demonstration to the Commissioner that the district has made a good-faith effort to hire licensed or certified personnel, and has been unable to find them. Persons employed under waivers must demonstrate that they are making continuous progress toward meeting the requirements for licensure or certification in the field in which they are employed."[18]

   Note: This basically allows practically anyone, especially with a college degree, to serve as a principal It also apparently assumes that the requirements for a principal can somehow be achieved in one year. It should be obvious that those who write such legislation have no real understanding of the role of a principal, and especially of the principal's responsibility for providing instructional leadership.

- *Florida*—"School district boards have authority to appoint persons to the position of school principal who do not hold educator certification."[19]

   Note: This law really is a travesty in that the state has basically abandoned its certification responsibility, allowing local school districts individually to determine the qualities, educational background, and training and experience required of a new principal. Florida essentially has allowed for sixty-seven different alternate routes within its borders.

Taken collectively, these four state examples, and others that could be cited, have recurring themes in their vision of what constitutes the background and training of a qualified school principal. These states seem oblivious to the roles and responsibilities of a building principal. Consider the common vision they espouse for a newly minted, alternatively certified principal:

- Anyone with a college degree can meet the requirements—and more power to the individual with an MBA.
- Previous teaching experience is not a consideration; apparently, the candidate will learn vicariously what teachers do and how students learn.
- It is not necessary to have a background in curriculum development; instructional strategies; working with diverse student populations, including students with special needs and English language learners; child growth and development; monitoring teacher efficiency and effectiveness; and engaging parents and the community. There is no concern that this new principal will not be accepted and have credibility as the school's instructional leader.

Regrettably, the backdoor entry for this new breed of alternatively certified principals has been rapidly widening, and over the past decade there has been a large infusion of these "principal pretenders." A major reason for this growth spurt can be directly attributed to the ill-advised School Improvement Grants (SIG) initiative, which holds the potential for significant teacher replacement, school closures, and conversions to charter schools. In all four of the initiative's models, discussed further in Chapter Fourteen, the principal must be replaced. Consider that the SIG initiative has a plan to identify five thousand low-performing schools over the next several years. Hence there may be a need to identify and place five thousand principals. This is a disturbing development because it can be predicted that a significant number of these replacement principals will come through alternate certification routes, with no previous experience working in public schools.

What is the rationale behind appointing individuals with no school or classroom experience as leaders in schools with students who have the greatest academic needs? This question gains importance when it is considered that other individuals with no background or training—alternatively certified—will be assigned as teachers. It would almost appear that there is a plan in place to ensure that disadvantaged students, with the greatest academic needs, in our poorest communities, have the least qualified teachers and leaders! What are these school reform zealots thinking?

Further, placing more alternatively certified principals in schools has serious implications for teachers—what can be expressed as "collateral damage." At a time when teachers are under pressure for greater accountability—and when such initiatives as "pay for performance" for student outcomes are driving state legislation and local education policy —high-quality and validated processes of teacher evaluation need to be in place. Without question, one of the major players in the evaluation of teachers is the building principal, whose role has significantly expanded as states and school districts have begrudgingly come to the realization that a state test, administered once each year, cannot be the sole factor in teacher evaluation. Nor can the test alone provide validation for merit pay consideration. As a result, the principal's role is gaining new currency in the evaluation of teachers.

The principal is gaining greater acceptance as the final arbiter in assessing the effectiveness of the classroom teacher, as the individual who makes recommendations for continuance of employment, as a central decision maker in recommending tenure, and as a key participant in determining performance pay considerations. The significance of the principal's role in teacher evaluation should point to the problems inherent in appointing alternatively certified principals, particularly when one considers what an educational leader, the principal, "needs to know and be able to do." Consider that it is incumbent on principals to be recognized "educational connoisseurs"—having a working knowledge of the art and science of teaching, understanding the skills that constitute good teaching, and possessing the acumen to recognize when good teaching is or is not present. These connoisseurs are instructional leaders who are able to assess the teaching and learning process; who are conversant with good classroom practice; and who can dissect all aspects of a teacher's repertoire, including lesson planning, methods for engaging students, instructional modalities, curriculum development, knowledge of subject matter, and the ability to individualize instruction.

These skill sets cannot be learned in corporate board-rooms or in administrative positions outside of education. They can only be learned and honed through experience teaching in a classroom setting, over some appreciable period of time. It borders on lunacy to allow individuals with zero classroom experience to provide instructional leadership to teachers and oversee student learning. It seems even crazier when such individuals are placed in our nation's poorest schools and with our most disadvantaged students.

Diane Ravitch offers further insight into the misplaced emphasis on alternatively certified principals:

> It is crucial that principals have prior experience as
> teachers and understand what good teaching is
> and how to recognize it . . . People with so little
> personal understanding of good instruction—what
> it looks like, how to do it, and how to help those
> who want to do it—are likely to rely exclusively
> on data because they have so little understanding
> of teaching. This is akin to putting a lawyer in
> charge of evaluating doctors or a corporate
> executive in charge of evaluating airline pilots.
> Numbers count for something, but on-site
> evaluation by an experienced, knowledgeable
> professional should count even more.[20]

At a time when there is a growing national emphasis on teacher accountability and paying teachers for performance, it becomes imperative that principals—who bear the major responsibility for evaluating teachers—have well-developed instructional expertise and have a high degree of credibility with the teachers whom they are evaluating. It seems likely that classroom teachers will experience distrust, frustration, and despair when their very employment and career status is to be determined by individuals "posing" as principals. They will become further exasperated if they are supervised and evaluated by individuals who lack a critical understanding of what constitutes the art and science of good teaching, and of how students learn and develop. Evaluations, made in such a vacuum, can only serve to

- Heighten teachers' anxiety about their professional future
- Decrease teachers' trust in those who are responsible for imposing such untrained principals on them
- Enhance the potential for significant litigation concerning teacher layoffs and terminations based on evaluations administered by alternatively certified principals
- Hasten individual teachers' decisions to leave the profession

This is not a time to look for quick fixes in school administration, creating "openings" for individuals from other work environments to suddenly emerge as school principals. If we are truly committed to improving our schools, advancing student learning, and developing a high-quality teacher workforce, then we need to place a premium on accomplished principals in all of our schools. We must demand more intensive preparation for and mentored induction of principals, ensuring that they will be steeped in instructional leadership skills. In turn, we would expect that such accomplished educational leaders—educational connoisseurs rather than misplaced surrogates—will apply their expertise to increase teacher efficacy and enhance student learning.

Chapter Three

PERFORMANCE PAY FOR TEACHERS: SEPARATING MYTH FROM REALITY

President Obama and Secretary Duncan have made performance-based accountability, including merit pay, a cornerstone of their education reform agenda. The pay-for-performance (PFP) movement has been accelerated by exhortations from corporate CEOs that educators must be held accountable for student outcomes. This has resulted in a chorus of support, which now includes approval from state legislatures and local school boards.

It is important to point out at the outset that teachers do, in fact, expect to be held accountable for their instructional abilities and for progress in student achievement. The conundrum for teachers, in accepting greater accountability, is that they cannot accept an evaluation model—with an impact on their very livelihood—that will be based on one annual state standardized test in reading and mathematics. Nor are they interested in being held accountable in the context of corporate models of accountability, which simply do not represent the educational environments in which they work.

It is time, as PFP advances, to separate some of the myths from reality. I recently had the opportunity to coauthor an editorial on PFP, which was published by *Education Week* as its online "Commentary Editorial" (April 12, 2012). Certain parts of the commentary that follows are gleaned from my editorial, along with some newer insights. Let's start by exposing some of the myths:

MYTH 1: PERFORMANCE PAY IS A HALLMARK OF THE BUSINESS COMMUNITY

An educator should be paid for his or her results, corporate barons insist, just like they are. Yet the business management literature is filled with warnings about plans for doling out incentives that rely heavily on quantitative rather than qualitative measures of good performance. W. Edwards Deming, a highly regarded management expert who helped shape twentieth-century views on effective management, admonishes those obsessed with quantitative measures: "Businesses seeking to improve quality and long-term performance should do away with standards, eliminate management by numbers and numerical goals, and abolish merit ratings." These measures encourage employees to focus on short-term results. Deming continues: "Management by numerical goals is an attempt to mandate, without knowledge of what to do, and in fact is usually management by fear!"[1]

Quite contrary to the continuing rhetoric of the business community advocating a model of PFP for teachers, it seems that businesses actually do follow Deming's advice. A May 2010 Economic Policy Institute (EPI) report estimates that only one in seven employees in the private sector is covered by a bonus or merit plan, which accounts for just a fraction of total compensation.

The EPI report further dispels the myth: "Although payment for professional employees in the private sector is sometimes related to various aspects of their performance, the measurement of this performance almost never depends on narrow quantitative measures analogous to test scores in education."[2] The report adds that "private-sector managers almost always evaluate their professional and lower-management employees based on qualitative reviews by supervisors; quantitative reviews are used sparingly and in tandem with other evidence." The report concludes with a strong and cautionary message concerning the use of quantitative measures to gauge and reward performance: "The national economic catastrophe that resulted from tying Wall Street employees' compensation to short-term gains rather than longer-term (but more difficult-to-measure) is a particularly stark example of a system design to be avoided!"[3]

So let's review what appears to be the common thinking: the business literature assails performance pay, and businesses use it only sparingly. And yet education should adopt performance pay as a centerpiece of reform. It's dizzying logic, but at least we have some insight into the thought process that doled out obscene bonuses to the executives who lost billions of dollars and brought our national economy to the brink of disaster.

Teachers are essentially being asked to submit to a corporate model of accountability—a model that it is not even widely used in the corporate sector. And considering the recent track record of corporate America, can anyone really blame teachers if they are not rushing to accept an account-ability approach from such a flawed segment of our society?

MYTH 2: RESEARCH SUPPORTS PAY FOR PERFORMANCE FOR TEACHERS

There is a dearth of research that supports paying teachers beyond their basic salary to improve teacher efficacy and student performance. At the same time, a broad body of research indicates that PFP might actually do damage, with teachers perceiving a threat to their livelihood because of the narrow method of measuring their abilities. PFP has been documented as compromising goodwill and cooperation among teachers because it creates competition for a small amount of money, often resulting in an "I'm out for myself only" attitude. The resulting loss of necessary collaboration and communication may hinder student success.

In addition, consider the findings of the National Center on Performance Incentives, commissioned during the George W. Bush administration. Researchers Patrick Schuerman and James Guthrie at Vanderbilt's Peabody College—where the study was funded—concluded that "there is no conclusive evidence on the power of financial awards in promoting more effective teaching and evaluating student performance, or on the long-term effect of perfor-mance awards on the supply of effective teachers."[4]

Three recent and highly visible studies support the find-ings of the National Center on Performance Incentives:

- The study of the New York City public schools teacher bonus program

- The first scientific study of performance pay in the United States, conducted in Tennessee by Vanderbilt University in partnership with the Rand Corporation
- The study of the Chicago Public Schools Teacher Advancement Program, initiated when Arne Duncan, the current secretary of education, was superintendent of the Chicago Public Schools

I describe each in more detail in the paragraphs that follow:

- The New York City public schools conducted a three-year study from 2008 to 2011, during which time the school district distributed $56 million in performance bonuses to teachers and other school staff members. Weighing evaluation data and surveys, the study found that *the bonus program had no effect on student test scores, on grades on the city's A-through-F school report cards, or on the way teachers did their job.* The study found that most schools distributed the bonuses equally to all staff members. But even where schools rewarded some teachers more than others, there was no positive impact on student performance. Teachers reported that improving as teachers through professional development activities and seeing their students learn were bigger motivators than a bonus.[5] Proponents of PFP should take this attestation by teachers into particular consideration when seeking to force this model of accountability on teachers.

  Of particular note is that the performance bonus plan in New York City was the brainchild of Mayor Bloomberg and then-chancellor Joel Klein, who have

been nationally recognized as leaders in the PFP movement. Not surprisingly, in 2011—and $56 million
later—the city abandoned its teacher bonus program.

- The Vanderbilt University study took place from 2006
  to 2009, with volunteer participation by math teachers
  in grades 5 through 8 in the Metropolitan Nashville
  Public Schools. The study's question was, "If teachers
  know they will be rewarded for an increase in their
  students' test scores, will test scores go up?" Researchers
  found that the answer to that question is no—*bonuses
  alone do not help teachers work harder to see student test
  scores rise.*[6]

  This comprehensive Vanderbilt study is considered the most rigorous study of performance-based
  teacher compensation ever conducted in the United
  States. Nevertheless, the findings have fallen on deaf
  ears, and there continues to be a national agenda to
  promote PFP.

- The Chicago Public Schools study, conducted by
  Mathematica Policy Research, began during the 2007–
  2008 school year when Duncan was superintendent
  of that city's school district. During that school year,
  Chicago's Teacher Advancement Program (TAP) was
  implemented. This program's multiple steps included
  increased teacher development and an incentive plan
  whereby teachers were paid more when their students
  did better on standardized tests. Under the program,
  payments to teachers in the experimental group aver-
  aged $1,100 for teachers in schools in their first year
  of implementation, and $2,600 for teachers in schools
  in their second year.

Results from the Chicago study, released in June 2010, were based on students' math and reading test scores. *There was no evidence that TAP improved student performance when results were compared with those of a group of similar schools that did not use the system.*[7] Not surprisingly, in 2011 Chicago abandoned TAP.

The Chicago experience and related findings are of added significance when we consider that TAP's main architect was Duncan, who now holds the highest national office in public education—and who continues to be one the most vocal national advocates of PFP.

The results of these studies add to a growing body of evidence nationwide that pay-for-performance bonuses for teachers that consist only of financial incentives have little to no effect on student achievement. Against such a backdrop of negative results for PFP initiatives, the advocates continue to insist on moving forward with PFP and seem to be unwilling to consider changing direction in regard to legislation and policy. William Mathis and Kevin Welner offer a strong warning to Secretary Duncan and other national leaders promoting PFP: "The federal government can contribute to our schools more effectively when policy makers in the Department of Education seek and embrace research-based solutions—even when the research contradicts the politics or prevailing ideologies of the day." The authors conclude with a caveat that "selective research [should] not be used for post-hoc justification for pre-determined ideological positions."[8]

MYTH 3: TEACHERS WILL BE POSITIVELY MOTIVATED BY THE ADDED FINANCIAL INCENTIVES PROVIDED BY PAY-FOR-PERFORMANCE INITIATIVES

Let's look more closely at the question of motivation. The reality is, teachers are not motivated by their involvement in PFP plans, and such involvement may lead to outcomes that are counterproductive when it comes to student academic improvement. Richard Rothstein, one of the authors of the EPI report, confirms this problem: "[PFP plans] base their judgments on narrow statistical indicators. That approach can result in unintended consequences as workers game the system or because of perverse indicators in the plan." He offers the following example: "When the former Soviet Union set shoe-production quotas, factories responded by producing larger numbers of smaller shoes. The smaller shoes were useless to consumers, though."[9]

This example has relevance for school reformers when it is considered that statistical indicators, incorporated in standardized state test results, drive our accountability system. State tests basically hold all teachers and students to very low standards of proficiency in reading and mathematics. Such standards allow teachers to reach desired performance results, but what these tests require of students pales in comparison to the more comprehensive and difficult skill sets that students will need to compete in a global society. Is this the type of misguided motivation we want to impose on our nation's teachers? One can only hope that this is not the case.

Regrettably, in the growing movement to advance PFP for teachers, we have seen a perverse motivation—on the part of several teachers and administrators—resulting in several school districts' being cited for extreme instances of cheating on state standardized tests. In such instances teachers and principals have been accused of changing students' answers on tests and falsifying test reports. This reality has become a national issue and has spawned a national debate as to whether there needs to be an effort to improve test management and security—or a push to scrap high-stakes tests altogether.

The dilemma inherent in the cheating scandals may be best captured by "Campbell's Law"—attributed to Donald Campbell, who developed the concept in the 1970s: "The more any quantitative social indicator is used in social decision making, the more subject it will be to corruption pressures and the more apt it will be to distort and corrupt the social processes it was intended to monitor."[10] This law—when applied to the ill-advised use of students' scores from a state assessment administered once each year—may well explain, but not justify, the aberrant behavior and motivation of some educators.

MYTH 4: STANDARDIZED TEST SCORES REPRESENT AN EQUITABLE AND RESPONSIBLE WAY TO EVALUATE TEACHER PERFORMANCE

There is a growing body of evidence that the use of standardized testing to measure teacher performance, or to make other high-stakes personnel decisions, is flawed in many ways, having the potential to create an uneven playing field for teachers. Even the more recent "value-added modeling" initiative—which essentially measures a teacher's effectiveness over time, after adjusting for some student and school characteristics, and which has been portrayed as a more effective and equitable way to measure a teacher's impact on student academic growth—has been seriously questioned. Rothstein brings these points into clear focus through his cogent warning, which is imbedded in the EPI report: "There is broad agreement among statisticians, psychometricians and economists that student test scores alone are not sufficiently reliable and valid indicators of teacher effectiveness to be used in high-stakes personnel decisions, even when the most sophisticated applications such as value-added modeling are employed."[11]

Linda Darling-Hammond addresses the issue of equity in using standardized test scores to assess teacher effectiveness. She offers two main points. First: "Test scores—even when using fancy value-added models—reflect much more than an individual teacher's efforts, including students' health, home life, and school attendance, and school class sizes, curriculum materials, and administrative support, as well as the influence of other teachers, tutors and specialists." She adds a very important caveat: "These factors differ widely in rich and poor schools." Second: "Teacher ratings are highly unstable . . . teachers who rank at the bottom one year are more likely to rank above average the following year than to rank poorly again. The same holds true for teachers at the top." Her succinct point: "If the scores truly measured a teacher's ability, these wild swings would not occur." The summary point for Darling-Hammond's introspective review of the fairness in using test scores to evaluate teachers is direct and concise: "These test scores largely reflect whom a teacher teaches, not how well they teach . . . This is true even when statistical measures are used to 'control' for student characteristics."[12]

"Whom a teacher teaches" is very significant when addressing the issue of equity for teachers in relation to any evaluation model that provides pay for performance and has job security implications. Any such model must consider the composition of a teacher's classroom and other pertinent factors, including the number of special education students, the number of English language learners, the teacher-pupil ratio, the number of students eligible for free or reduced-price lunch (considered a proxy for poverty), the type of community the school serves—affluent or poor—and rates of student absenteeism. Teachers whose classrooms contain students with a number of the aforementioned characteristics are at a disadvantage when competing with teachers who do not face the same set of circumstances. Teachers who work in schools in low socioeconomic communities face a number of challenges that essentially do not exist in the more affluent communities—placing them at a distinct disadvantage in any PFP model of accountability.

The issue of fairness to teachers is also evident when it is considered that state tests are generally administered only in reading and mathematics, which raises immediate questions about any pay-for-performance system that purportedly applies to all teachers in the school system:

- If only the teachers who teach reading and mathematics can receive monetary compensation (because these are generally the only subjects in which states are testing), how are other teachers in other subject areas (social studies, art, music, foreign languages, physical education, science, civics, social work, bilingual education, and so on) to be eligible to compete for additional monetary compensation?

- Conversely, if alternate assessments are used to evaluate the "other-subject" teachers, how is this an equitable outcome for those teachers whose compensation is directly related only to standardized test results?

- What, if any, consideration is given to special education teachers, whose accountability and reward structure cannot be tied directly to any standardized testing instrument—given that they have students with a wide range of disabilities, including autism, significant physical and cognitive disabilities, and mental retardation? Have the advocates for standardized testing forgotten the scope and purpose of the Individuals with Disabilities Education Act (IDEA), which emphasizes the central role of a school's planning and placement team in treating each special education student's learning needs on an individual basis—determining the least restrictive environment and what constitutes appropriate testing for each student? How can a special education teacher be held accountable, and receive additional compensation, based on a standardized testing model that is foreign to any concept of individualized instruction and is in direct conflict with the intent of IDEA?

- Have the PFP advocates considered that linking teacher compensation and job security to standardized test scores will exacerbate the problem of teachers' not wanting to teach in schools with the greatest needs? Do they understand that working in such schools places teachers at a significant disadvantage when compared to teachers in more affluent schools and districts?

- Has anyone considered the reality that the students who take part in the standardized testing program have no interest in their individual results, which have no bearing on their classroom grades, promotion to the next grade level, or graduation requirements? Is there an understanding that these tests have no real currency with students, unlike teacher-administered classroom tests, advanced placement tests, PSATs, SATs, the ACT, or International Baccalaureate examinations—all of which have individual consequences for students? Is there any concern given to the extreme unfairness of a PFP system that relies on a standardized testing platform whereby standardized tests have high stakes for the teachers involved but zero meaning for the students taking them? Is anyone even considering this serious disconnect?

A FINAL WARNING ABOUT PAY
FOR PERFORMANCE

The authors of the EPI report neatly sum up the problems with pay for performance I have described throughout this chapter. I would urge everyone who is advocating PFP as a means to enhance teacher effectiveness—legislators, school board members, district office leaders, and policymakers— to stop and consider the EPI cogent warning: "Adopting an invalid teacher evaluation system and tying it to rewards and sanctions is likely to lead to inaccurate personnel decisions and to demoralize teachers, causing talented teachers to avoid high-needs students and schools, or to leave the profession entirely, and discouraging potentially effective teachers from entering it. Legislators should not mandate a test-based approach to teacher evaluation that is unproven and likely to harm not only teachers but also the children they instruct."[13]

Chapter Four

TEACHER BASHING: TO WHAT END?

Educational consultant and public educator advocate Jamie Vollmer has referred to the increasing vitriolic attacks on public schools as "the practice of bashing public schools as a blood sport": "Sensational headlines publicize half-truths, statistics are used out of context, false comparisons are made between past and present, public versus private, us versus them, and test results are reported in the worst possible light." Vollmer admits that bashing public schools has been going on for many years, but he offers a caustic warning that this time the attacks on public education are very different: "We are witnessing a campaign to annihilate the emotional and intellectual ties that bind the American people to their public schools."[1]

It is against this unfair and demoralizing backdrop that the critics of public education erroneously identify the classroom teacher as the main contributor to what they perceive as the malaise of public schools. This continued bashing of the teaching profession has had a dramatic impact on teachers' psyche and caused them to seriously question the extent of public support for, and commitment to, their hard work and conscientious efforts. The critics—often federal officials, corporate and foundation leaders, legislators, and school board members—show little awareness that education doesn't take place in a vacuum.

The external factors that can dramatically affect teacher efficacy and student learning are multifaceted, profound, and often intractable: poverty, unemployment, homelessness, inadequate housing, poor health care, single-parent households, and neighborhood gangs—to name just a few. Clearly, teachers have no control over these realities, which a significant number of students bring with them to the classrooms daily, and which are inextricably linked to student performance.

Poverty's significant impact on student achievement was clearly identified in the landmark 1966 federal study the Coleman Report—one of whose core findings was that family background has twice the influence that schools do over student achievement. Richard Rothstein's research confirms this finding: "Decades of social science research have demonstrated that differences in the quality of schools can explain about one-third of the variation in student achievement. But the other two-thirds is attributable to non-school factors."[2]

Rothstein goes on to take strong issue with a number of major teacher reform initiatives: "It would inappropriately undermine the credibility of public education if, in such an economic climate, educators were blamed for their failure to raise student achievement of disadvantaged children. *Indeed, educators should get great credit if they prevent the achievement of disadvantaged children from falling further during this economic crisis.*"[3]

That teachers are not the core component in improving student achievement is articulated by none other than President Obama, who has offered this insightful observation: "I always have to remind people that the biggest ingredient in school performance is the teacher. That's the biggest ingredient within a school. But the single biggest ingredient is the parent."[4] The operative phrase in the president's statement is "within a school." Without question, the classroom teacher has a profound and lasting influence on student achievement, but, as President Obama notes, there are other influences that need to be recognized and addressed, including the role of the parent.

Also arguing that teachers and schools alone cannot be held accountable for closing the student achievement gap is secretary of education Arne Duncan, who has said: "It takes more than a school to educate a child. It takes a city that can provide support from the parks department, health services, law enforcement, social services, after school programs, non-profits and businesses and churches."[5] Secretary Duncan's observation clearly addresses a multifaceted approach to closing the achievement gap that goes well beyond what schools and teachers alone can offer from the confines of the schoolhouse. It is also gratifying to note that the secretary's comments reflect a keen awareness of the guiding principles of community education, and its central role of coordinating municipal services in supporting school reform initiatives.

Even though it is encouraging that these two national leaders understand that teachers and schools alone are not responsible for improving student achievement, there continues to be an obsession at the federal level with advancing legislation and policies—especially through the Race to the Top (RTT) initiative—to support implementing pay for performance for teachers, removing teacher tenure, and reducing teacher seniority. The continued RTT "push" seems antithetical to the statements of both Present Obama and Secretary Duncan, which support a view that the problems of school improvement far transcend what takes place in a classroom.

I hope, in the future, we will see more of a commitment to the words that national leaders espouse—and see those words, in turn, match their actions!

DO OUR NATIONAL LEADERS TRULY SUPPORT TEACHERS?

It is important for our national leaders to gain credibility and trust with teachers. Teachers must see a viable commitment to a legislative and policy direction that they can support, and not just empty verbiage to alleviate their concerns and frustrations. To emphasize this point, consider the feedback Secretary Duncan received following an effort on his part to reach out to teachers. In 2011 the secretary published an open letter to teachers in honor of Teacher Appreciation Week[6] expressing a "deep and genuine appreciation for what you do," and further stating that "you deserve to be respected, valued and supported." Although the secretary is to be commended for communicating with our nation's teachers and articulating his vision to "invest in teachers and strengthen the teaching profession," his message received some very unenthusiastic responses.

The cool reception to his message was captured in the comments *Education Week* received following the publication of Secretary Duncan's open letter, which bring into clear focus teachers' high level of discontent, their lack of trust, and the angst they feel toward Secretary Duncan and his administration. Excerpts from selected teacher responses follow, clearly making the case that teachers are tired of words that are not accompanied by supportive action[7]:

- "As long as you trust billionaires and business minded people to make decisions for professional educators, you do not value teachers nor students. Until your actions show respect, your words are of no value" (G. K. Pruett).

- "Stop asking us to join your agenda. Trust that we might have some better ideas from our experiences and ask us if you can have the wisdom of our collective voice. But you are not interested in our wisdom . . . so we are not interested in yours" (Mrs. Van Houten).

- "It is well and good (and the right thing) to appreciate teachers this week. However, the best policy is to appreciate teachers all year by working to incorporate our views, ideas and insights into policy . . . Can you now, in action, demonstrate that you hear and respect us by promoting policies we can stand behind, celebrate and rally behind? I hope so" (Jason Flom).

- "Until Duncan acknowledges the experiences and priorities of teachers and parents, and reverses his destructive policies, this sort of superficial rhetoric will have little impact on our views of his administration . . . More and more, teachers are being held accountable for things over which they have no control. Fully 2/3 of the factors that influence learning are outside of a teacher's school control. Yet, you persist in using evaluation protocols that rely mostly upon scores that are incapable of differentiating among causal factors. Therefore I find your polite words hollow and disingenuous" (Leonie Haimson).

These responses, among many others, sent a strong message to the secretary as to the high level of frustration and disdain that teachers feel toward the policies his department and the Obama administration are imposing. Although his open letter was well intentioned, the responses it generated conveyed teachers' desire to be consulted with—and to be appreciated for their work. The time for words is over—teachers now want supportive action from leaders in Washington DC.

STATE POLICIES AND DISTRICT POLICIES: SHAMING AND BLAMING

Another area of major concern for teachers is the expanding movement in states and school districts to consider making public their student scores on state standardized tests as well as individual teacher rankings. This is yet another cause of great consternation and heightened frustration within a teaching force that already feels besieged by a growing negativity concerning their worth and efforts. In addition, such public exposure sends a false message that teachers alone bear the responsibility for student achievement. Such a message completely puts aside any consideration of the myriad and complex social, economic, and family background factors that have a bearing on student growth and development. In effect, the advocates of such public pronouncements completely ignore a wide body of social science research—cited earlier, but worth repeating—suggesting that "differences in the quality of schools can explain about one-third of the variation in student achievement. But the other two-thirds is attributable to non-school factors."[8] How many times can those promoting public rankings of teachers ignore well-documented research?

To publicly hold teachers accountable for a single set of scores, from a test administered once each year—illogically implies that the other 179 days of classroom instruction can truly be summed up in this number. Bill Gates, reacting to the release of New York City's test scores and rankings—which were based on small sample sizes and whose calculations had large margins of error—offered a strong cautionary message: "Developing a systemic way to help teachers get better is the most powerful idea in education today. The surest way to weaken it is to twist it into a capricious exercise in public shaming."[9]

"Shaming" has no place in any individual's assessment, and actually is counterproductive in improving teacher competence. Furthermore, such shaming will become a major deterrent in recruiting and retaining teachers.

It is and will continue to be very difficult for teachers to function as successful professionals in a climate in which teacher rankings are publically displayed—especially rankings based on incomplete data that have significant margins of error—and in which the results of one test determine a teacher's job security. An anonymous, oft-used quotation, "The beatings will continue until morale improves," brings into clear perspective a pervasive, underlying belief that if teachers are continually reminded of their failings and short-comings, they will somehow miraculously do better!

Until policymakers awaken to the reality that meaning-ful reform can only occur through working with teachers in a climate of trust, confidence, and support, any efforts are doomed to fail.

Chapter Five

GETTING TEACHER REFORM
BACK ON TRACK

There should be no question that reform within the teaching profession is a critical component in improving teacher effectiveness, which in turn contributes to enhancing student achievement and closing the achievement gap. However, there are no quick fixes or "reform du jour" initiatives to address the complexity of what is needed in the reform effort. Nor are there any magic bullets in addressing how and the extent to which reform initiatives should be developed and implemented. Teachers can see right through many reform initiatives imposed from afar, a number of which have little chance of effecting change and tend to be met with the teacher response: "This too shall pass!"

The specific recommendations offered in this chapter have the potential to transform the teaching profession, elevate the status of teachers, engage them in the change process, and advance student learning. I have been personally involved in the development and implementation of several of the recommendations presented. The others are crafted based on my extensive observations of teachers at work and on personal interactions with teachers and administrators. These observations and interactions have afforded me the opportunity to gain, over many years, a clearer understanding of what is needed to improve the professional standing of teachers as well as the conditions and circumstances of their daily classroom experiences. I believe that these recommendations, if considered and implemented, will gain wide acceptance by teachers, have major credibility with legislators and policymakers, and have a longer-term impact on improved student performance.

A Word About Cost

Without question, a majority of these recommendations will have significant financial implications. We can dramatically minimize the cost factor, however, if we reconsider the present fiscal priorities driving our national education reform agenda. As referenced earlier, in providing a new vision for federal involvement in school reform, the Race to the Top (RTT) and the School Improvement Grants (SIG) programs alone have provided billions of dollars to initiatives that are less promising—offering competitive financial support to a small group of selected states. Consider the impact these extensive dollars could have if they were applied directly, on a national scale, to teacher preparation, induction, career development, and salary enhancement.

Rather than committing our national fiscal resources to improving teaching—which has been widely recognized by many researchers and in numerous reports as the *in-school*

variable that is most important to school improvement—
we have instead spread our dollars thinly among a limited
number of states, having a minimal impact on schools and
students. Tavis Smiley and Cornel West, in their recent book
The Rich and the Rest of Us, bring the RTT financial commitment into the broader context of our national priorities.
They discuss a meeting held with West (one of the book's
authors) and Secretary Duncan. At the meeting the secretary
argued that the Obama administration had made closing the
achievement gap in America a top priority—and added that
the RTT funding commitment served as a sign of that pri-
oritization. Consider how blunt West was in his retort to
the secretary: "I know that you are all break dancing over
this $4 billion dollar commitment, but Afghanistan gets $4
billion every day. So militarism trumps any case of poverty
and poor children. That's the country's priorities and how
warped our priorities are."[1]

West's rebuttal to Secretary Duncan brings into serious
question the degree to which our nation truly places education—especially the education of our poorest children
—high on its list of priorities. There is no question that
to close the achievement gap will require a huge commitment of national and state resources and funding—which
should first and foremost be directed at ensuring that
every classroom has a competent teacher. Unless and until
that commitment is made, our nation will face a widening
achievement gap, and will have difficulty recruiting and
maintaining the quality teacher workforce necessary for student improvement.

The following recommendations are presented without
major concern for the funding implications. It is my strong

belief that the necessary funds will become available once our nation comes to grips with the need to elevate education to a much higher priority—and to recognize teachers as the core in-school component of school and student improvement.

RECOMMENDATION 1: DRAMATICALLY INCREASE TEACHER SALARIES

There are those who will question the wisdom of highlighting teacher salaries as part of the first recommendation for reforming the profession. Many believe that teacher compensation is a minor factor, and that if it is raised at all as a consideration, it should be buried in an inconspicuous part of any reform document. I unabashedly disagree with such thinking and feel that teachers, like any other professionals required to meet advanced college degree requirements, should be compensated in a way commensurate with their training and expertise. It borders on disgraceful that the national average starting salary for teachers, as reported in a 2010 national salary survey, is approximately $30,400. Compare that with the $43,675 for computer programmers; $44,688 for accountants; and $45,700 for registered nurses.[2] Although the reported starting salary for a teacher is already extremely low, the hidden reality behind this average is that there are several states that still offer starting salaries in the mid-$20,000 range—which places such salaries very close to the national poverty level for a family of four! Marc Tucker, president of the National Center on Education and the Economy, offers a vivid depiction of the substandard wages paid to teachers: "Not only do teachers make markedly less than other occupations requiring the same level of education, but census data shows that teachers have been falling further and further behind the average compensation for occupations requiring a college degree for 60 years."[3] Tucker adds: "We do little or nothing about starting salaries that will not permit a young family to support a small family in the style to which college graduates are accustomed in this country. In most places, teaching continues to be a dead-end career, with no routes up except those that lead out of teaching."[4]

Considering the long history of depressed teacher compensation, it is difficult to comprehend how it will be possible to raise standards for teacher preparation programs, recruit high-quality teacher candidates, require even more stringent teacher licensing and certification standards, and place added accountability measures on teachers.

My bold, timely, and necessary recommendation for addressing this long overdue issue, which has been relegated to the "graveyard" of teacher reform considerations, is as follows: over the next five years, raise beginning teacher salaries to a *minimum of $55,000*, and develop salary schedules that will *allow experienced, competent teachers to earn up to $150,000*. In fact, there are studies and reports that address the need to raise teacher salaries to levels similar to those I propose. Of particular note is a study released in 2010 by the highly respected consulting firm McKinsey & Company, which offers a sobering conclusion that merits the attention of all legislators and policymakers: "The country could raise top-third new hires from 14% to 68% by paying new teachers at least $65,000 and offering a maximum salary of $150,000."[5]

My personal recommendation not only takes into consideration the studies and reports previously mentioned but also draws on my own experience. In 1986, during my tenure as Connecticut's commissioner of education, the state-level Education Enhancement Act (EEA) was passed, which raised the minimum starting salary for all teachers to $30,000 (experienced teachers could earn from $75,000 to $85,000). Consider that this nationally recognized teacher salary breakthrough occurred twenty-six years ago and allowed Connecticut to be in the enviable position of having no difficulty recruiting top teacher candidates and retaining a highly competent teacher corps.

To move this proposed salary initiative forward, I recommend that the federal government provide major funding grants to states over a ten-year period. The level of funding for each state should be based on the wealth and need status of the state. In turn, states and local school districts should be required to provide some level of funding to match the federal grants. Both the federal and state grant commitments should be tied to ensuring that a state's poorest communities receive the highest priority for funding increased teacher salaries.

Again, some may question from where this "new" funding will emanate. At the risk of being redundant, I remind the reader that refocusing the RTT and SIG monies would be a great first step in providing a funding source for raising teacher salaries. In addition, reevaluating national funding priorities—and significantly elevating the importance of funding for education—should serve to reallocate existing funds to boost teacher salaries. The ultimate funding determination will be contingent on whether there is a national will to treat the state of public education and its teachers as a matter of national urgency.

An important argument for this urgency, embedded in several national reports, is that a well-educated citizenry is imperative to the future economic standing of the nation. In regard to this point, consider that numerous reports abound that reach the same basic conclusion: improving student learning, closing the achievement gap, and reducing the dropout rate will result in trillions of dollars of increased productivity in the economy in the long term. To realize these desired outcomes will necessitate a *continuously* improving system of public education, with such improvement inextricably linked to the quality of the nation's teaching force. A strong case can be made that increasing teacher salaries—acknowledging the pivotal impact of teachers in school improvement—will reap major national economic gains in the future.

RECOMMENDATION 2: FOCUS TEACHER EVALUATION AND SYSTEMS OF ACCOUNTABILITY ON SKILL SETS AND CLASSROOM OUTCOMES

Teacher accountability is at the forefront of national school reform.

Without question, dramatically raising teacher salaries will rightly place an increasing burden of accountability on teachers in regard to improved student achievement. The real issue for teachers will not be accountability in general, but rather *how* they are evaluated and held accountable for their work. Continuing down a path on which only student scores on state-administered tests determine teacher competence completely misses the totality of the teaching and learning experience. I predict that teachers will fully accept accountability if the evaluation of their performance is comprehensive in nature, encompasses the many and diverse skill sets embedded in teacher competence, and is conducted through rigorous and ongoing assessments by skilled evaluators ("educational connoisseurs"). The criteria for teacher assessment and accountability should include

- Demonstrated academic student outcomes as evidenced by classroom work
- The quality of lesson planning
- The ability to individualize instruction
- Working knowledge of one's subject or subjects
- Understanding of curriculum development
- The ability to diagnose both class and individual learning problems, and provide prescriptions for improvement
- Effective classroom control and management
- Sensitivity to children's needs
- The ability to address the individual needs of students with special needs and English language learners
- Continuous self-improvement through professional development
- Use of research-based pedagogical strategies

If the results of state tests continue to be a factor in teacher assessment, they should be used only as one specific measure within a comprehensive system—and should be subsumed in the totality of the skill sets that are representative of teacher performance. Further, a high-quality system of teacher evaluation should not focus only on assessment outcomes, but should encompass rich and instructive feedback from those conducting the evaluation. Such feedback should be given in a timely manner, should provide teachers with concrete recommendations for improvement, and should be accompanied by the tools necessary for honing follow-up improvement strategies.

RECOMMENDATION 3: STRENGTHEN THE ROLE OF PRINCIPALS AS INSTRUCTIONAL LEADERS

It is imperative that principals, who are generally the main evaluators of teacher performance, be trained as instructional leaders who have a strong working knowledge of the various skill sets identified in the previous recommendation, and who are adept at having intellectual discussions with teachers on improving classroom instruction. The importance of the principal's role in teacher evaluation cannot be overstated. It becomes a significant issue when teachers lack confidence in the principal's ability to analyze their teaching prowess—especially when the principal plays such a central role in regard to tenure decisions and job security.

It becomes incumbent on schools of education to dramatically change their program of study for those aspiring to become principals, moving away from their long-standing focus on school management, finance, and the development of administrative skills. Although these skill sets are important, the overemphasis on such skills has minimized the extent to which future principals are trained as leaders of student learning instructional strategies and enhanced teaching practice. I recommend that as part of a principal preparation program, every candidate should spend at least one semester as a full-time intern under the tutelage of a "master principal" who is a recognized leader in teacher supervision and evaluation. There is no real substitute for this type of on-the-job training in gaining a greater understanding of what constitutes high-quality teacher evaluation.

One of the complexities of placing the major burden on principals to serve as instructional leaders, and as the primary evaluators of teacher performance, is the time factor. As the school's leader, the principal is responsible for a variety of duties and has fluctuating demands. Even the best-trained principal, however well intentioned, may not always find the time necessary to devote to classroom supervision and teacher evaluation. This reality suggests the necessity of developing other models to support the principal in this important part of his or her work.

RECOMMENDATION 4: USE PEER EVALUATORS TO SUPPORT TEACHER EVALUATION

One of the models for supporting principals in the realm of teacher evaluation that merits serious consideration is *peer evaluation*, which would allow teachers who have been trained in supervision and evaluation methodologies to conduct classroom observations of other teachers. Many outstanding classroom teachers are widely respected in states and school districts for their classroom expertise and ability to continually achieve positive gains in student achievement. These teachers generally have great credibility with their colleagues as exemplars of the teaching profession. There are numerous examples across the nation in which such teachers have developed the requisite skills to provide direct assistance to principals in the evaluation of fellow teachers. Teachers, functioning in such a capacity, generally have instant standing with their colleagues in that they "have walked in their shoes" and have a deep understanding of, and appreciation for, what constitutes excellence in teaching. With appropriate training and preparation in the skill sets necessary to function as evaluators, peer teachers can become a major asset to a school's principal in a coordinated effort to improve and enhance the quality of teaching.

Without question, the use of teachers to evaluate their colleagues will necessitate discussions, and possibly negotiations, with state departments of education, local school boards, and teachers' unions to address related certification issues and concerns as well as contractual agreements. Before state officials, school board members, and teachers' union officials put their heads in the sand to avoid addressing this innovative approach to teacher evaluation, we need to remind them of the following: they can't point to the difficulty of having the school principal alone carry on the intensive requirements of high-quality and validated teacher evaluation—and in many cases question the ability of the principal to adequately perform this task—while at the same time "closing their minds" to having expert teachers assist in meeting demands for greater teacher accountability.

In regard to my own experience with peer evaluation, I had the opportunity to implement such a program statewide in 1987 while I was serving as Connecticut's commissioner of education. The previously referenced state-level EEA included the component of peer evaluation for all beginning teachers. The legislation allowed for, and funded, an intensive program for highly competent teachers to be trained, over the summer months, as peer evaluators. As a result, each first-year teacher was evaluated over the course of his or her initial year by six different peer evaluators, who used the same protocols to make their evaluation recommendations. All such evaluations were given to the new teacher within one week of each classroom observation. The results of the six evaluations were collated at the end of the year, with copies given to the new teacher, and basically constituted the teacher's official evaluation for the first year of teaching.

This was a very powerful evaluation tool in that if a teacher's composite evaluation was negative, that evaluation would take precedence over a superintendent's recommendation for certification. In many cases, however, teachers receiving negative evaluations were allowed to continue for a second year with the same type of peer evaluation and with additional support and mentoring. The outcome was that a large number of teachers continued into a second-year probationary period. These teachers were given extensive support, and often showed great improvement. A significant number of them were retained in their position. The peer evaluators were also given a state-funded stipend for their work in this area. Overall, the peer evaluation program proved highly successful, and it made excellent feedback available to beginning teachers in what traditionally is a difficult entry year in the profession.

RECOMMENDATION 5: ESTABLISH TEACHER EVALUATION CERTIFICATES

I also recommend that states consider implementing a specific certification for the position of teacher evaluator—other titles could be teacher examiner, evaluator of teaching practice, or teacher specialist. The individuals seeking such a designation should have long-term experience as successful classroom teachers. This certification should also be available to presently employed principals, superintendents, and other educational staff—with the one consistent requirement being previous exemplary teaching experience. It is highly advisable that presently employed teachers and administrators take on this new responsibility as a full-time position. This consideration is imperative in that the evaluator's position will be demanding, and the related responsibilities should not be compromised by other duties and distractions.

This specialized certification should also be available to recently retired administrators and other educators. Again, the one consistent requirement for these candidates would be documented evidence of competence in teaching. It is possible to consider allowing retired individuals to assume this responsibility on either a full- or part-time basis, as they will not necessarily be involved in other school-related duties that impinge on their time and commitment.

Achieving this certification would require taking a state-administered examination to determine the extent to which individuals understand the elements of exemplary teaching practice and how they can be measured in a classroom setting. In addition, the candidates for this certificate must conduct formal teacher observations and evaluations under the supervision of trained monitors. This specialized certificate should be valid for a period of only three to five years, with recertification required thereafter. This process will ensure that the teacher evaluators are up to date on current trends in teaching pedagogy and on other conditions that affect classroom teachers.

This initiative has great promise for improving teacher evaluation and providing greater verification of teacher competence in an age of increasing teacher accountability. Consider the valuable features of this type of certificate:

- Enhanced credibility for the evaluation process because "licensed" evaluators are performing the evaluations.
- Increased opportunities for exemplary teachers to use their skills and expertise in service to their colleagues, allowing them a new career path in their profession without their having to "jump" into an administrative position. Further, the potential exists for additional remuneration for having unique and highly desirable skills in teacher evaluation.
- Increased opportunities for recently retired educators to stay involved in their profession by using their extensive background, training, and experience to provide expert assistance in teacher evaluation and in designing follow-up strategies to improve teacher performance.
- Welcomed assistance for principals in the realm of teacher evaluation, respecting the reality of the time commitment required to do an effective job in this area on an ongoing basis. The principal would remain

involved in teacher evaluation, continuing with classroom observations in coordination with the teacher evaluators assigned to his or her school. The key point is that the daily pressure of personally conducting evaluations—a task conflicting with the many other diverse responsibilities of the position—would be alleviated.

- Enhanced credibility of evaluators among classroom teachers, who would have a greater sense that those performing the evaluation are conversant with the teaching-learning process and have present (or very recent) experience as classroom teachers.

RECOMMENDATION 6: PROVIDE CAREER LADDERS FOR TEACHERS

Teaching as a profession is very limited in terms of its prospects for advancement, unless the teacher is prepared to leave the classroom and seek out an administrative-type position. The impetus for such a change is generally the need to increase one's salary: teacher salary schedules tend to be stagnant, and it takes many years of service to realize a "decent" level of remuneration. The reality is that teacher salaries also pale in comparison to administrator salaries. Even if teachers love their work and the daily contact with students, teaching represents for many a type of dead-end job in which their various skill sets are not likely to be recognized and rewarded. To address this conundrum, states and school district need to develop and implement teacher career ladders, which would give teachers the opportunity to expand their role outside the classroom in a variety of ways, such as by mentoring new teachers, functioning as curriculum specialists, leading professional development programs, serving as peer evaluators, coaching experienced teachers in need of assistance, and assuming various leadership positions. The type and level of engagement in these diversified roles would be contingent on a teacher's skill sets, areas of interest, and willingness to spend time away from his or her classroom assignment.

It is further recommended that teachers who elect to participate in career ladder programs remain rooted to their classroom assignments and provide their extensive experience and background to assist other teachers in the school on a part-time basis (for example, one to two periods per day or one to two days out of each week or month). A schedule of this type will allow teachers to engage in out-of-classroom experiences in specialized support services, which will benefit the entire school. In turn, this will allow for a greater sense of personal self-actualization, which is not always possible within the confines of a classroom.

It is important that teachers initially participating in such an initiative retain their primary focus as classroom instructors, thereby maintaining their standing and credibility. It is possible that over time some of these specialized skill sets may result in a full-time position. This will depend on both a teacher's willingness to leave the classroom and a school or school district's commitment to maximizing the level of support the teacher is providing to the school and students.

A career ladder program also affords teachers the opportunity to receive additional remuneration for taking on their expanded role. An important consideration in this type of "salary adjustment" is that the teacher is being rewarded for his or her skill sets. This does not fall under the heading of pay for performance; rather, teachers are compensated for their expertise, their knowledge base, and the level of schoolwide support they provide.

This type of initiative will also necessitate additional funding to supplement salaries, and to pay to have extra teachers on staff to cover the classrooms of teachers who are on out-of-classroom assignments. Developing schedules in which no more than one teacher is away from a classroom at any one time can minimize this cost. Possibly having one to two additional full-time teachers on staff can also assist with scheduling issues and concerns.

RECOMMENDATION 7: CONDUCT A WHITE HOUSE CONFERENCE ON "LISTENING TO THE VOICES OF TEACHERS"

Consider a letter that Barbara Weaver, a teacher, sent to Secretary Duncan in response to his open letter to teachers (discussed in the previous chapter). In her letter, Weaver voices her frustration, questions the secretary's sincerity in actively engaging teachers, and offers him a challenge: "You say you want to 'work with' teachers to undo the wrongs of NCLB. However, I get no sense of how you propose to include us from this article. What, exactly, do you propose to do to create an individual dialogue with the nation's teachers?"[6]

President Obama would send our nation's teachers a loud, clear, and welcoming message on the subject of opening a dialogue if he would personally convene and participate in a daylong conference on teachers' recommendations for school reform and the advancement of their profession. Secretary Duncan and leaders of Congress should also attend this conference. The conference would serve its greatest purpose if it were held well in advance of the reauthorization of NCLB. I further recommend that the audience consist of a significant majority of practicing classroom teachers. Although it is expected that teachers from both the American Federation of Teachers and the National Education Association would be in attendance, it would serve a greater purpose if extensive efforts were made to have a large number of unaffiliated teachers in attendance. This effort would defuse the arguments of those who might suggest that teachers' unions, and not rank-and-file teachers, controlled the proceedings.

There needs to be a clear message to the Obama administration that teachers feel completely isolated from the national school reform discussions—and from the dialogue that has an impact on their very profession and ultimately their livelihood. To support this contention, the MetLife Survey of the American Teacher reported that "69% of teachers do not believe their voices are heard in the debate on education." The survey also noted that "teachers (67%) and principals (78%) believe that increased collaboration among teachers and school leaders would have a major impact on improving student achievement."[7]

Anthony Cody, a National Board Certified Teacher, coordinated a teacher letter writing campaign to President Obama in which teachers expressed their frustrations about their lack of inclusion at the school reform table. Referring to the many letters sent to the president, Cody summarized: "Teachers have been treated like immovable objects in need of enormous policy levers to move us, but these messages reveal a profession hungry for change. That change will be released when we are engaged as active partners in the process, as these letters offer."[8]

Cody's reference to teachers' being treated like "immovable objects" brings to mind the dilemma of living the "life" of a puppet whose very "existence" is fully dependent on a puppeteer's pulling its strings to allow movement of any kind. Using the puppet analogy, it is possible to juxtapose the dilemma of teachers who feel that their professional lives are being controlled by far-removed "puppeteers"—Obama administration officials, federal and state legislators, corporate and foundation bigwigs, and policy gurus. These puppeteers, rather than engaging teachers as active players in school reform, are content to allow teachers to participate only when they pull their strings!

The Obama administration must clearly understand that school reform cannot exist solely in the realm of government and legislation, and that one cannot transform schools vicariously. To be successful, those crafting policies and leading reform efforts must have the classroom experience that enables one to gain a true understanding of what is needed to improve public schools.

To further the argument for greater teacher engagement in school reform, the Obama administration must be reminded that there is no other profession that would allow "outsiders" to set the terms, conditions, and expectations for the work its practitioners do. After decades of failed school reform initiatives—imposed by those far removed from the education profession—we must ask, How many more misguided and ill-conceived reform efforts will be tolerated before the reality sinks in that decision making power in school reform must be returned to the teachers in the classrooms?

The Obama administration has a great opportunity—by convening a White House conference—to display its commitment to and resolve in welcoming teachers as full and respected participants in the discussions on school reform. This initial gesture would be well received, and would heighten the Obama administration's credibility with and perceived responsiveness to the millions of teachers who proudly serve our nation's students.

RECOMMENDATION 8: REFORM TEACHER PREPARATION PROGRAMS

There has been a long-standing debate surrounding the quality of college and university preparation programs for teachers, and about how beginning teachers are basically left on their own as they assume their initial teaching assignment. Similar important considerations arise in any profession in which college or university preparedness is essential to providing individuals with the requisite skills, knowledge base, attributes, and level of acumen to be successful in their career choice. In education, major concerns are low standards for entry into such programs; a lack of focus on subject matter; an overreliance on teaching methods courses; limited periods of time devoted to student teaching experiences; questionable expertise of "master teachers" supervising student teachers; little, if any, review and understanding of brain research and the implications for student learning; and minimal graduation requirements to assess readiness and competencies. Taken individually and collectively, these concerns are exacerbated when beginning teachers begin their career with minimal support and assistance to help offset the shortcomings in their preparation program.

- In fairness, it is important to note that over the last fifteen to twenty years there has been a concentrated effort by many colleges and universities to improve their teacher preparation programs in an attempt to address the various concerns just cited. In addition, the National Council for Accreditation of Teacher Education (NCATE) has raised its standards for accreditation, and has been more aggressive in monitoring and validating the progress of preparation programs. Although there is some level of optimism that improvement is taking place—based on colleges and universities' policing their own programs and NCATE's taking a more assertive stance in determining the programs to which it provides accreditation—there are counterbalancing realities at work:

   It remains relatively easy to gain acceptance to teacher preparation programs. This is supported by data from the College Board, which reported in 2008 that "when high school graduates going on to college were asked what their intended major was, those who had decided on education scored in the bottom third on the SATs. Their combined scores in mathematics and reading came in at 57 points below the national average."[9]

Another finding of the McKinsey study discussed earlier further exposes the problem of low standards: "Teaching as a career . . . lacks prestige in the United States. More than half of teachers are trained in schools with low admission standards; many accept virtually any high school graduate who applies."[10]

Low scores and entry standards not only demonstrate that teacher preparation programs are not attracting the best students but also send a clear message as to the low academic caliber of those entering teacher preparation programs directly from high school. This reality is a critical issue for the future, and supports the essential need to elevate the status of teachers, increase their salaries, and give them a "voice" in their profession.

- A significant number of colleges and universities have apparently turned a deaf ear on calls to reform their teacher preparation programs. This is especially true at state schools, which enroll the vast majority of education majors. The main reason behind this is that having minimal entry requirements allows the universities to enroll students who are less academically prepared and ensures a continuous flow of tuition funds—resulting in teacher preparation programs' having the dubious distinction of being referred to as universities' "cash cows"!

- State departments of education, which generally bear the major responsibility for monitoring—and in many cases approving—teacher preparation programs, do not have the necessary number of experienced staff or the financial resources to adequately oversee these programs. This becomes a critical issue when it is considered that many states have, over the years, been accused of simply "rubber stamping" teacher preparation approvals. Quality control at the state level is conspicuous by its absence.

- The majority of states require candidates applying for teacher certification to achieve a passing score on the Praxis test—developed by the Educational Testing Service—or on another commercially developed test. The difficulty in determining the extent to which these tests can serve as a national proxy for teacher readiness lies in the reality that each state sets its own bar for passing the required test. There is virtually no national consensus as to what constitutes teacher readiness; instead, each state makes its own determination, and many states set the passing bar very low.

  A 2012 article in *Education Week*, "Teachers Pass License Tests at High Rates," supports this concern: "The average scores of graduating teacher-candidates on state required licensing exams are uniformly higher than the passing scores set for such exams. The pattern appears across subjects, grade levels, and test instruments . . . raising questions about the rigor and utility of current licensing exams."[11] Dan Goldhaber, a research professor at the University of Washington, concluded the following in reviewing the *Education Week* data: "If there's not a lot of variation in the performance of graduates by a university, it could mean that education seems to set a lower bar for institutions than other professions."[12] Goldhaber brings into clear focus that teacher preparation programs have a much lower set of expectations for their applicants compared to similar

programs in other professions. Serious concerns therefore surface that state licensing exams are of little value
in validating a teacher candidate's preparedness for
entering the profession. Other issues and concerns arise
when we consider that the fifty states cannot agree on
what beginning teachers should know and be able to
do, instead defining expectations on a state-by-state
basis.

We can learn valuable lessons by reviewing and
analyzing the work of the National Board for Professional Teaching Standards (NBPTS), which has developed high standards, comprehensive assessments, and
common passing scores for recognizing accomplished
teaching. Everyone must meet the same criteria, regardless of the state in which he or she resides. There are no
exceptions! It seems both rational and urgent to build
on the example NBPTS has set—to develop national
standards and assessments to authenticate the readiness
of the nation's future teachers.

The time is now to address the issue of teacher preparedness and the process of induction into the teaching
profession. Before presenting my specific recommendations,
it is important that I describe briefly the context in which
they were formulated. The recommendations are based
largely on my personal experience in transforming teacher
education during my tenure as Connecticut's chief state
school officer from 1983 to 1993. In addition, I have spent
many years monitoring the various issues and concerns
that have "held back" the necessary and substantive changes
necessary for the reform of teacher preparation programs.

Once again I must reference the Education Enhancement Act, passed by the state legislature during my tenure as the chief state school officer in Connecticut. The component of the legislation that received the greatest national attention was the Beginning Educator Support and Training Program, which had a bearing on teacher preparation and induction.

The reforms that were achieved in Connecticut—parts of which have been altered over the years—still have currency and merit serious consideration, especially in relation to preparing a teacher workforce. In the specific recommendations that follow, in some cases I have personally changed or added to the component parts of this reform model to make it more relevant for addressing the preparation and induction of teachers. The recommendations in this list as well as Recommendation 9 are presented in a particular order, starting with candidates entering the preparation program and continuing through the initial year of teaching:

Specific Recommendations

1. Prior to entering a teacher preparation program, which in many states can be as early as the junior year of college, a candidate should have a minimum grade point average of a B– in work at the college level. In addition, the candidate must pass a state-administered basic skills exam in reading and mathematics. The key point here is that passing such an exam is not the same as ultimate success in the program, but rather indicates that the candidate is literate in basic skills—an absolute prerequisite for anyone considering a teaching career!

In Connecticut, in the early years, it was very discouraging to see a fairly large number of candidates fail the exam—which really was a confirmation of the low entry requirements for the universities. The good news is that after the initial years, when the "word got out," students became more serious about their academic pursuits.

2. All candidates must major in the subject they plan to teach. Elementary school candidates must provide evidence of having taken extensive course work in both reading and mathematics. It makes consummate sense that if a candidate is planning to teach science—or any other subject—then he or she must have a solid knowledge base in that subject.

3. All teacher preparation programs need to require a bachelor's degree plus one year of postgraduate work. This recommendation is not new—indeed, it was originally made by the Holmes Group, a major teacher preparation reform initiative created in the mid-1980s —but it is still not the norm among states. This extra year is critical because it allows teachers the time to take a full component of courses in their subject area, develop a strong background in pedagogy and learning theory, and engage in intensive student teaching experiences.

4. State departments of education must carefully ensure the presence of high-quality and instructive student teaching experiences, respecting the fact that such experiences are an integral part of a state's certification process. States must see to it that expertise and a record of accomplished teaching are required to be designated as a supervising teacher—to be allowed to monitor the

development of student teachers and to provide the support and assistance necessary to enhance their development. This isn't often the case. Indeed, there exists a long history in public schools of supervisory teachers being selected at random, with little specific attention paid to their ability to perform the necessary functions.

5. It is recommended that all master teachers, those supervising student teachers, be trained and certified as such by their respective state departments of education. This should include a rigorous selection process and an intensive summer training program. Master teachers should also be provided with a state-funded stipend based on the number of student teachers under their tutelage.

    The important task of selecting master teachers should not be left to the discretion of local school districts, unless there is a comprehensive training program, including a rigorous selection process, approved by the state.

6. All states must require that on graduation from a teacher preparation program, and as part of the certification process, candidates should be required to pass a state-administered examination in the subject area for which they are seeking certification. Elementary school candidates should take a comprehensive examination with a focus on reading and mathematics. Furthermore, the examinations developed in Connecticut required candidates to view and critique videos of teaching practice, and I recommend that elementary school candidates be required to identify strengths and weaknesses in similar presentations, indicating how

they as teachers would personally engage with the situations depicted in the videos.

RECOMMENDATION 9: IMPROVE TEACHER INDUCTION INTO THE PROFESSION AND ON-THE-JOB TRAINING

Once granted certification, a beginning teacher should be given a one-year probationary certificate, with advancement to the next level of certification—generally a provisional certificate, good for an additional three years—contingent on satisfactory evaluations from the school district's superintendent and the peer evaluation team (referenced in Recommendation 4). Beginning teachers who are considered "borderline" at the end of the first year should be given an initial year, with increased classroom support, and should remain in the probationary category.

Each first-year teacher should be assigned a mentor teacher who is trained, and who possesses a state certification, to function in this role. The mentor teacher should also be a practicing classroom teacher, rendering the support and guidance provided more credible as well as affording the beginning teacher the opportunity to observe the mentor teacher in his or her own classroom setting. Mentor teachers should be given a state-funded stipend in exchange for their time and expertise.

Tenure decisions should not be made until a beginning teacher has satisfactorily moved through the probationary and provisional certifications—a process ranging from four to five years, depending on how long it takes a beginning teacher to move through the probationary phase. This entails an extensive period of time available for observation, supervision, and evaluation of a teacher's prowess in the classroom prior to the granting of tenure. The reality is that tenure itself should not be seen as the problem in ensuring quality in classroom teaching—which is often the case for those who are cynical about the teaching profession. Rather, the problem lies in the absence of high-quality supervision and evaluation during the initial four to five years of teaching. As was referenced earlier, it is extremely rare for teachers to awaken on their first day of tenure and suddenly become incompetent. All of the harbingers of incompetence were generally observable during that four- to five-year period, if only those responsible for recommending tenure had been paying attention!

Improving teacher preparation and induction into the profession cannot be accomplished in a piecemeal fashion, instead requiring a comprehensive, coordinated, and integrated approach. Taking such an approach will require the support and commitment of all of the "players," including schools of education, school district personnel, and state departments of education. The model presented in this chapter provides an all-inclusive framework to energize the dialogue necessary to begin the important work of reforming the preparation of tomorrow's teaching force.

A FINAL WORD

The recommendations presented herein are based on my conviction that *the teacher is the center of the education universe*, and that the teacher is the most important in-school contributor to student achievement. I hope that each recommendation, given its depth and scope, will be given serious consideration, and will serve as a launching pad for a national discourse on the types of reform strategies that can propel the teaching profession into the more positive future it deserves. Such a future looks bright for improved student achievement and closing the academic gap.

Part Two

CHARTER SCHOOLS: HELPING OR HURTING SCHOOL REFORM?

Chapter Six

CHARTER SCHOOLS: A DREAM DENIED

There is an inherent contradiction between the scope and purpose of charter schools today and the initial purpose for which they were intended. This is an important point to consider, and one that has been lost on the Obama administration, legislators, and policymakers in their steadfast encouragement of the growth of charters.

The champion for the charter movement was the nationally recognized teachers' union leader Albert Shanker, who at the time was president of the American Federation of Teachers. In the late 1980s Shanker had a vision of allowing small groups of teachers to come together and form their own schools, removing all bureaucratic red tape and union rules and affording teachers an opportunity to develop—on their own terms—curricula, schedules, governance structures, and instructional and teaching strategies. The desired outcome was that the innovations and successful interventions developed to improve student learning and teacher efficacy would serve as models that could be emulated in traditional public schools (TPSs).

Shanker's vision was to create living laboratories for teachers to experiment and try out new pedagogical strategies to improve teaching and learning. To this end, he was successful in impressing on educational leaders in Minnesota his concept of a new charter school movement. Shanker envisioned that such schools would serve as incubators for meaningful school change, initiated and implemented by those closest to the conditions influencing teaching and learning—classroom teachers. The ultimate outcome was that Minnesota opened the nation's first charter school in 1992, incorporating many of the components of Shanker's vision.

The birth and subsequent life span of the charter school movement encompass two sobering realities. First, the movement was initiated by a leader in a teachers' union who envisioned the potential to "turn teachers loose" and live their dreams. Today, paradoxically, charter school proponents identify such unions and their leaders as the main critics of the charter movement. Second, the initial purpose of charter schools has been corrupted from one of informing and supporting public schools to one of placing charters in the position of competitors to public schools. This new resolve was never a part of Shanker's vision; it has moved charters completely off-course in relation to the original, intended direction; it has resulted in public schools losing needed funding and resources; and ironically it has resulted in the very organization that championed its cause withdrawing its support for advancing charters.

In a 2009 *Education Week* op-ed titled "The Charter School Express," Western Michigan University education professor Gary Miron and community organizer Leigh Dingerson, who has coauthored a book on charter schools, point to the way charter schools have veered from their original mission: "The charter school idea was to create better schools for all children, not to divide limited public resources across parallel systems that perform at similar levels and suffer similar breaches in accountability."[1]

In her 2010 article for the *New York Review of Books* titled "The Myth of Charter Schools," Diane Ravitch also notes the significant change in direction from what Shanker envisioned more than two decades ago, and comments on where the charter school movement is drifting in the twenty-first century: "Today, charter schools are promoted not as ways to collaborate with public schools but as competitors that will force them to get better or go out of business. In fact, they have become the force for privatization that Shanker feared."[2]

Where did it all go wrong? How did what was intended to be an innovative vision to empower teachers become what is today a competitive and at times combative exercise in school reform?

The initial change in direction can be attributed to a growing concern with the nation's low student achievement levels in economically disadvantaged communities, and the lack of progress in closing the achievement gap between minority and nonminority students. The consensus of far-removed school reformers was that the schools alone were responsible for these outcomes, and that greater opportunities had to be provided to students in low-performing schools. To this end, several administrations (from the first Bush administration to the Obama administration); governors; state legislators; and policymakers offered charter schools as alternatives to traditional public schools—completely putting aside the original vision for charters.

The early 1990s ushered in the age of competition, pitting public schools against charter schools. The result was that rather than put more resources and funding into public schools with the greatest needs, state legislatures and local school boards allowed these much-needed resources and funding to become part of a competitive contest with the newly minted charter schools. Instead of focus being placed on those schools with the largest number of students with significant demonstrated academic needs—schools for which a greater return in terms of student achievement was possible—the end result was a dramatically watered-down effort in which resources were diverted to a tiny number of schools and students.

More recently there has been a growing concern among educators and parent groups that charters' competition with public schools has escalated, with greater involvement by for-profit charter operators and the infusion of significant fiscal resources into charter schools from the foundation world.

Ravitch emphasizes this escalation by bringing to light *New York Times* articles that make the case that "charter schools have become the favorite cause of hedge fund executives." She points out that when Andrew Cuomo wanted to access fiscal support for his gubernatorial campaign, he made overtures to Wall Street executives, including the executive director of Democrats for Education Reform. Hedge fund operators who provide extensive fiscal support to political campaigns dominate this latter group—and have also provided major financial assistance to the charter school movement. The reality here is that certain of the titans of Wall Street have focused their attention on funding charter schools—which is driven, not for educational purposes—but rather for a profit motive.[3] Ravitch offers a chilling conclusion about the emergence of foundations and hedge fund managers in the charter movement: "What we're seeing is an effort to impose deregulation and the free market into education. The fascination with charters among philanthropists and Wall Street has diverted the attention away from tackling the hard problems of public education."[4]

It would take a very naive individual to reach a conclusion that the recent and expanded interest of Wall Street and its hedge fund managers in funding charter schools represents their magnanimous commitment to assisting low-performing students. Rather, the logical deduction is that they are driven by the profit motive, for themselves and for their investors. The inclusion of these new external and extensive funding streams may very well fulfill Shanker's feared prophecy of the privatization of American public education.

Taken to its extreme, greater privatization would result in public schools' bearing the main responsibility for our nation's students who would be left behind. Unlike public schools, private schools play by their own rules and have great flexibility in student selection. Conversely, public schools (rightly) have no alternative but to accept all students, including those with the greatest needs: low-achieving students, students with special needs, English language learners, and those living with the debilitating impact of poverty. In a future characterized by greater privatization, charter schools will begin to look more like private schools. It seems likely that they will use lottery systems extensively, working only with "enlightened" parents who fully understand the selection process. Such a future direction for the charter movement, with its devastating and draining impact on public schools, would violate all of the underlying democratic principles inherent in our nation's commitment to its system of public education.

"WAITING FOR 'SUPERMAN'": DO CHARTERS OUTPERFORM TRADITIONAL PUBLIC SCHOOLS?

The growing interest in charter schools received a substantial boost with the release of the documentary film *Waiting for "Superman"* in 2010, which was highly supportive of charters—basically portraying them as the salvation for students with the greatest academic needs.[5] The film received an inordinate amount of national attention, being featured on NPR and such programs as *Oprah* and *Good Morning America*. In addition, NBC conducted an Education Summit in New York City—which I personally attended—that was like a pilgrimage to charter schools. It should also be noted that the summit received substantial funding from corporations and foundations committed to expanding the charter movement, which once again raises significant concerns and questions about the long-term financial motivation behind such commitments.

Waiting for "Superman" is really the story of a loss of hope in the public schools and how charter schools came to be viewed as the holy grail of school reform. The documentary is a highly distorted, unfair, and disparaging depiction of our nation's public schools and educators. Yet it is hard to look away from the small, vulnerable faces of the children whose educational odysseys are highlighted in the movie—as they and their parents anxiously wait to see if they are lottery picks for a coveted charter school. It's also hard not to sympathize with the fiercely protective yet seemingly politically powerless parents who struggle mightily to ensure that their children get a high-quality education.

The low-performing public schools represented in the film absolutely have to be fixed, and they deserve major attention, resources, and assistance. There is no denying this reality. The problem is that Davis Guggenheim, the film's director, provides the viewer with only one part of the landscape of our nation's public schools—giving the impression that the worst 5 percent of our nation's schools is representative of the other 95 percent.

Guggenheim makes no effort in the film to identify and tell the numerous stories of public schools in low-income neighborhoods that have—in spite of immense negative odds—completely turned themselves around and are recognized as models of school improvement. The film's director pays no attention to the fact that numerous charter schools are unsuccessful and in many cases have been closed. Rather, the film's strong message is that charter schools alone represent the future of school reform, provide the greatest opportunities for improving student achievement, and should proliferate across the country.

The focus that Guggenheim places on charter schools has not been lost on President Obama and his secretary of education, Arne Duncan, both of whom have become strong advocates of the charter movement. The Obama administration's high level of support is evident in the Race to the Top and School Improvement Grants programs, each of which prioritizes funding in large part based on a state's commitment to expanding charter schools, as required in the program's regulations.[6] As a postscript to this discussion of the Obama administration's commitment, it is important to point out I have personally heard educators express their frustrations and concerns in regard to the inordinate number of visits President Obama and Secretary Duncan have made to charter schools—while at same time spending only limited time in public schools. In fact, this concern was expressed early on, when Obama's first school visit as president was to a charter school in Washington DC—an action perceived by the education community as dismissive of the reality that 95 percent of our nation's students attend TPSs.

One really has to wonder if those who label charter schools as the answer to school reform pay any attention to the recent evaluations of charter schools, the majority of which highlight poor results for charters when compared to TPSs. The most comprehensive, longitudinal study of charter schools was conducted in 2009 by the Center for Research on Education Outcomes (CREDO) at Stanford University. The study examined the performance of charter schools compared to TPSs across fifteen states and the District of Columbia. The results of this study have major significance and have a high level of credibility, given that the study encompassed 70 percent of charters nationwide. The main Credo Study findings, summarized by Eileen O'Brien and Chuck Dervarics, follow, which should give pause to those advocating a greater proliferation of charter schools: "While some charters do better than the traditional public schools . . . , the majority do the same or worse. Almost one-fifth of charters (17 percent) performed significantly better (at the 95 percent confidence level) than the traditional public school. However, an even larger group of charters (37 percent) performed worse in terms of reading and math. The remainder (46 percent) did not do significantly better or worse."[7]

A simple mathematical exercise will reveal that 83 percent of traditional public schools do as well as or better than charters! Taken collectively, these validated findings do not present a success story for charter schools, instead raising serious questions about charter schools' value and impact as part of a comprehensive school reform strategy.

It is also important to point out that the National Alliance for Public Charter Schools (NAPCS) has reported that eleven states have not been included in any major charter studies other than those revealing national data, such as National Assessment of Educational Progress scores. In seven other states, only "snapshot studies" provide a glimpse of the impact of their charter schools. In summary, in eighteen states there has been no real effort at research, and therefore no evidence to creditably represent the extent to which charters in those states—which have made little, if any, effort to test their charter students—have had an impact on improved student achievement. Nor is there any conclusive comparison between charter schools' achievement levels with those of TPSs in these same states.[8]

According to O'Brien and Dervarics, NAPCS also "expressed particular concerns that some states with large numbers of charter students . . . do not have a single longitudinal student-level study published, and charter students in some states with significant recent growth in charter schools . . . have not received rigorous study at all."[9] The reality is that the one available comprehensive, longitudinal, and credible evaluation of charter schools (CREDO's study) clearly sends a message that traditional public schools more than hold their own in advancing student achievement when compared to charter schools. In addition, the NAPCS report already referenced exposes the fact that a significant number of charter schools have undergone extremely limited, if any, evaluations to determine their impact on student achievement.

Consider the reality, as noted earlier, that only 17 percent of charter schools do better on student achievement than traditional public schools, thereby representing a potential that for every hundred new charter schools, only seventeen charters will exceed the achievement levels of traditional public schools. In addition, based on the CREDO study's findings, it can be projected that 37 percent will do worse! Conversely, for every hundred new charters, eighty-three traditional public schools will have better or equal achievement outcomes. One can only conclude that the charter school proponents, in this age of accountability for public dollars, are satisfied with a "return on investment" of

17 percent, and are prepared to accept a "loss on investment" of 37 percent.

Considering such overwhelming statistical projections, there is a genuine need to question the rationale behind committing additional federal and state dollars to expand the number of charters as a major school reform strategy, when such commitments have an impact on only a relatively small number of schools and students. Margaret Raymond, director of CREDO and the study's lead author, offers this statement reinforcing the reality of the projections referenced earlier: "If this study shows anything, it shows that we've got a two-to-one margin of bad charters to good charters. That's a red flag."[10]

We have to wonder what Secretary Duncan was thinking when he informed states—with no documented evidence to support his edict—that "states with charter-friendly laws and policies will get first crack at awards from his $4.35 billion Race to the Top Fund."[11] In reality, his pronouncement resulted in marching orders for governors and legislators to jump on the charter school bandwagon.

It is increasingly difficult to comprehend the escalating commitment to, and major infusion of federal and state funds into, the charter school movement in the absence of any supportive data as to its efficacy. This apparent "evidence avoidance" comes on the heels of NCLB, which required states, school districts, and schools to use only "scientifically based research" programs and initiatives in school reform efforts—a directive that appears 125 times in the legislation. Is it any wonder that educators and the general public are so suspicious of and cautious in accepting the constantly changing federal and state school reform mandates?

A concluding statement from the CREDO study realistically frames the present debate on charter schools' achievement results versus those of TPSs: "This study reveals in unmistakable terms that, in the aggregate, charter schools are not faring as well as their TPS counterparts. Further, tremendous variation in academic quality among charters is the norm, not the exception. The problem of quality is the most pressing issue that charter schools and their supporters face."[12]

Charter school advocates should consider carefully the significant issue of quantity over quality as they lead the movement to accelerate charter school growth. Regrettably, accelerated growth, regardless of achievement, has become the engine of change for these proponents of the charter movement. This commitment to growth is vividly reflected in the Center for Education Reform's annual ranking of state charter laws, which is, according to Miron and Dingerson, "silent on academic accountability or performance, but identifies the potential for unlimited growth as one of the four indicators of a strong charter law."[13]

The military saying "Damn the torpedoes, full speed ahead" seems appropriate to describe charter school advocates' unwavering resolve!

Chapter Seven

THE EQUITY PROBLEM

A number of significant equity issues and concerns pertaining to charter schools merit serious consideration as the movement accelerates its expansion. These include the following:

RACIAL ISOLATION

Racial isolation is greater in charter schools than in traditional public schools. A report by the Civil Rights Project at the University of California, Los Angeles, found that "racial isolation is even more prevalent in charter schools than in traditional public schools." The report also includes the "striking" finding that "charter school segregation levels for African-American students over the last two decades have outpaced steadily increasing public school segregation." The same report offers a strong cautionary observation: "Tying education stimulus to charter numbers unfairly pressures states to ramp up efforts to authorize and open charter

schools without considering the impact on racial and economic isolation of students."[1]

This greater racial isolation in charter schools compared to traditional public schools should serve as a wake-up
call to those advocates who are so aggressive in pursuing an
urgent expansion of charter schools with little concern for
the potential "collateral damage."

UNDERREPRESENTATION OF STUDENTS
WITH DISABILITIES

**Charter schools serve disproportionately fewer students
with severe disabilities than do traditional public schools.**
Thomas Hehir of Harvard University, a leading advocate for
children with disabilities and former director of the U.S.
Department of Education's Office of Special Education Programs, confirms this assertion based on his work in San
Diego, Los Angeles, and Boston: "Charters in some cities
educate only a miniscule proportion of students with mental
retardation in comparison with regular public schools." He
adds that this reality "undercuts the assertions by some that
charters are outperforming regular schools."[2]

That students with severe disabilities are underrepresented in charter schools is also very evident in the Denver
Public Schools. Cheryl Karstaedt, executive director of student services in the district, provides further insight into
this reality: "Our charter schools do serve kids with disabilities, and a number of them serve a high percentage of
students with disabilities. But, by an 'overwhelming' margin
those students have learning, speech-language or emotional

disabilities, which we would consider more in the mild–moderate range."[3]

A further review of the total enrollment of students with disabilities in Denver helps us grasp the magnitude of this issue. In 2008–2009 the school district's charter schools served 7,000 students, of whom 780 had one or more disabilities. Of that 780, only 2 had a severe disability! Karstaedt explains: "The result is a situation in which people assume that children with severe disabilities cannot be served in charter schools . . . And this is true, that charter schools are not necessarily set up to work with such students."[4]

Juxtaposed with the dramatic underenrollment of students with severe disabilities in charter schools, and the reality that charters are not necessarily equipped to meet the needs of these students, is the continuing equity commitment of the U.S. Department of Education in its continuing edict that any charter expansion must serve *all* students. In fact, the department added language to that effect when it published its final priorities for Race to the Top funding. If charter schools continue to maintain that they—like traditional public schools—are committed to educating all children, then they must clearly understand that *all means all*!

Of course, traditional public schools (TPSs) are accountable for educating, and welcome the opportunity to educate, the full range of students with disabilities, including those with the most severe disabilities. To offer a comparison of student achievement among such dissimilar populations is truly unfair, casting TPSs in a negative light. Rather, TPSs should be applauded and celebrated for their commitment to and accomplishments with students with special educational needs. TPSs truly embody "all means all," and offer equal educational opportunity for all students.

ENGLISH LANGUAGE LEARNER CONSIDERATIONS

Underenrollment of English Language Learners (ELLs) in charter schools is also a problem. A national report issued in 2010, *Schools Without Diversity: Education Management Organizations, Charter Schools and the Demographic Stratification of the American School System*, confirmed that "more than half of the charters enrolled far fewer ELLs than did their home districts."[5] It is also important to point out the suspect practice of comparing achievement data for ELL students in charters with those of ELL students in TPSs. For example, lawyers for an advocacy group for ELL students in Massachusetts circulated a brief showing that "ELLs are greatly underrepresented in the state's charter schools, and that those who do attend them have generally been in the United States at least four years." Further, the authors of the brief "equate time in the United States with an increased level of proficiency and surmise that ELLs at charter schools tend to be easier to educate than those in regular schools."[6]

In other words, how long an ELL student has been in the United States is an important variable when assessing academic achievement. Numerous studies confirm that the longer a student with limited English proficiency is in the United States, the better the student will perform in school. A direct consequence—which makes consummate sense—

is that as a student advances in learning and understanding English, his or her potential to do well on any assessment written in English increases.

It therefore becomes incumbent on anyone conducting a comparative evaluation of ELL students in charter schools and in TPSs to ascertain the amount of time each student in the study has been in the United States and enrolled in school. A related equity concern—in any comparative study—is the manner by which charter schools recruit, accept, and retain their ELL students. Again, charter schools, like TPSs, must be held accountable to the equity imperative of "all means all" in their student enrollment policies and practices.

ATTRITION

A significant number of charter schools have very high attrition rates. Consider that researchers, in conducting evaluation studies, seldom if ever present data on the number of students originally enrolled in the charter schools under review, along with the number of students remaining in the schools at the time of the assessments. This consideration is noted by Steven Wilson in a working paper for the American Enterprise Institute: "Student attrition policies in charter schools have as yet received little attention, but are comparatively easy to study and could have potent effects."[7]

Diane Ravitch offers a specific example of the impact of attrition in her critique of *Waiting for "Superman,"* highlighting the documentary's failure, in presenting a supposedly successful charter school, to bring to the viewer's attention the role of attrition in the "success story." In the documentary, director Davis Guggenheim portrays Geoffrey Canada as one of his heroes, citing Canada's development of the highly acclaimed Harlem's Children's Zone. However, Ravitch brings the glaring misrepresentation of success, never referenced in the documentary, to the surface: "It should be noted—and Guggenheim didn't note it—that Canada kicked out his entire first class of middle school students when they didn't get good enough test scores to satisfy his board of trustees."[8] How is it possible that the film's director could miss—or simply avoid—such an unconscionable action on the part of a charter school's director and board of directors, and still present this school as a success story to the public? If ever there was a case of attrition being used to elevate student achievement levels, this charter school wins the prize!

The "disappearing" populations of certain charter schools place TPSs at a serious disadvantage in comparative evaluations in that TPSs cannot summarily dismiss students who may drive their test scores down. The question of whether or not charter schools and TPSs are competing on a level playing field merits serious consideration in analyzing evaluation results for schools in both categories.

John Merrow, education correspondent for *PBS NewsHour*, in analyzing the student achievement data of a charter school study conducted for New York City in 2009, raised serious questions about the positive results reported by the study's lead author, Caroline Hoxby—results that Hoxby asserted could be generalized to other urban communities. Merrow offers the following observation: "As with all education research, caveat emptor is a good rule to adhere to. For one thing, nowhere in the published study does Hoxby reveal how many students went through eight years in charter schools. She does acknowledge that she did a fair amount of extrapolating." Merrow expresses his concern that the extrapolation of data results in an unfair representation of comparisons, using the analogy of a foot race to represent the unfair comparisons of charter schools to TPSs: "Think of an eight-mile road race in which only some runners ran the entire distance. Most however ran some portion of the distance—miles one through three, say, or miles five through seven. And then the race officials compiled the final standings by assuming that those partial race times would have been replicated over the full distance."[9]

Merrow offers his conclusion about the unfairness embodied in this way of generalizing test results: "If someone who ran only three or four miles of the course got a trophy, there'd be an uproar, but of course, statisticians, like Hoxby, are comfortable with drawing inferences about academic performance."[10] Merrow's analysis brings into clear perspective the importance of knowing when students enter charter schools, when they leave, the duration of their enrollment, and the manner in which their length of enrollment is factored into the final evaluation results. It also seems appropriate to expect evaluators to review the conditions and circumstances that caused students to leave their charter school prematurely.

One teacher's personal observation of the impact of charter school attrition on student achievement levels in her school district provides further insight into the importance of this issue. She noted that a charter high school in her school district had reported continuous and impressive growth in student achievement over time. She raised serious concerns as to the accuracy of these test score results, pointing out that in 2004 the charter high school had an enrollment of 1,200 students, and that by 2011 the enrollment had "plummeted" to 740 students. Her questions in regard to this dramatic loss in the charter school's enrollment over time again focus attention on the suspect nature of many charter schools' "success stories": "What's wrong with this picture? What value does this school bring if it is not helping the kids that really need it beyond being 'coached' out due to so called 'HIGH' standards . . . or behavior . . . really? . . . Or is it more, you're not cut out for our school, so get out? Just asking."[11]

It is also important to recognize the questionable attrition practices of the "no excuse" charter schools—which include schools in the highly recognized Knowledge Is Power Program. These are schools that steadfastly reject any explanations students give for their low achievement—including not accepting a student's excuse for failing to meet the school's high standards or complete a class assignment. In effect, the implication is that students who fail to adhere to the standards and who do not comply with required assignments can be summarily dismissed. Some of these schools also "quietly acknowledge" that it is their policy not to fill empty seats at midyear or above a certain grade level.[12]

Wilson captures the questionable nature of such policies: "If some students leave because they are struggling academically in the program or are unwilling to meet the program's unusual demands, the policy may yield a positive selection effect, such that the average test scores and college acceptance rates are higher than they would be if those students remain enrolled." Wilson adds: "Keeping vacant seats unfilled relieves the school of incorporating new students who have not benefitted from the program in prior years and are likely to perform at levels below their classmates."[13]

"WE TAKE THEM ALL!"

Jamie Vollmer, a business executive and owner of a highly successful ice cream business, at one point was a critic of public education but later underwent a dramatic transformation in his views. Vollmer explains that years ago, when giving an address to teachers on the shortcomings of public education and the importance of practicing total quality management in schools, he was interrupted by a teacher's question. The teacher wanted to know, "Mr. Vollmer, when you are standing on your dock and you see a shipment of blueberries arrive and those blueberries do not meet your triple A standards, what do you do?" Vollmer's immediate reply was: "I send them back." At this response the teacher sprang to her feet and offered her response, which became famously known as the "Blueberry Story": "That's right! You send them back. We can never send back the blueberries *our* suppliers send us. We take them big, small, rich, poor, hungry, abused, confident, curious, homeless, frightened, rude, creative, violent and brilliant. We take them with head lice, ADHD, and advanced asthma. We take them with juvenile rheumatoid arthritis, English as a second language, and who knows how much lead in their veins. We take them all, Mr. Vollmer! Every one. And *that's* why it's not a business. It's a school!"[14] This encounter transformed Vollmer's views of the public schools, and for the past twenty years he has been an avid supporter of public education in his books and presentations.

The truth is that public schools, by committing to educating all students all the time, have a commitment to equity that charters simply can't share.

Chapter Eight

CHARTER SCHOOLS: INNOVATIVE *AND* EFFECTIVE?

A significant problem surfaces when charter schools are presented as the wave of the future in advancing school improvement, resulting in a fast-paced rush to judgment as charter school advocates push to make charter schools part of a national school reform model. As one might expect, the issues, observations, cautions, and research findings presented in earlier chapters will serve to challenge the power of the charter movement, and indicate the urgency of any effort to slow down the charter movement's forward momentum.

Grover "Russ" Whitehurst, the assistant secretary of education in the second Bush administration and a highly respected researcher in the field of education, provides a direct and lucid argument against the push for a national charter school movement: "We have little evidence that a nationwide system of charter schools can succeed in providing good enough education to all children."[1] In another article, he adds: "I do not see the present evidence as suggesting it is time to throw in the towel on traditional public schools."[2]

Charter schools and innovation, to many, conjure up the same meaning. Charters do meet the basic definition of innovation, representing something new and different among strategies for school reform. Newness, however, is not in and of itself the condition necessary for meaningful school improvement. If innovation does not lead to desired outcomes, we must raise serious questions about the need for the innovation to continue, let alone accelerate its growth. Innovation, in this context, represents a serious conundrum for charter school advocates. Unless and until charter school advocates can demonstrate long-term and sustained improvement in student achievement, charter schools' effectiveness must be called into question and their expansion should be stalled.

Whitehurst perceptively offers this construct for assessing innovation: "Unless effectiveness is thought of as a central dimension of innovation, the current innovation zeitgeist will subject the nation to yet another era of fad and fancy in education rather than continuous improvement."[3]

Whitehurst further clarifies his concerns about innovation by referencing the position on innovation taken by the Knowledge Alliance—an organization engaged in providing tools, training, and assistance to school districts to support student improvement—"that we should turn the page on past efforts." He notes: "Surely all past efforts weren't ineffective any more than all efforts to 'break the mold' will work." Speaking to this latter point, he succinctly and dramatically cautions: *"Idiocy can masquerade as innovation."*[4]

CRITICAL QUESTIONS WE NEED TO ASK

Given these concerns about effectiveness and Whitehurst's cogent warning, it is imperative that we consider a number of urgent questions:

○ *Can charter schools be scaled up to constitute a national model for school reform?* The answer to this question is a resounding no! In 2011 there were approximately 5,600 charter schools serving approximately two million students.[5] These numbers represent the very slow growth pattern of charter schools, averaging 250 schools per year over a twenty-year period (from 1992 to 2011). While the average represents 250 schools per year, charter schools have shown a significant increase over the past several years. However, the growth of charters schools pales in comparison with the magnitude of traditional public school enrollment of over fifty million students in over 100,000 schools. Based on the growth pattern of charter schools to date as well as future projections, it would take a hoped-for "utopian age" for charters to approach the scale necessary to become a viable national force in school reform.

In addition, it is important to consider that the charter school movement has made inroads almost solely in large metropolitan areas or in urban communities, with minimal if any presence in suburban or rural communities. In particular, the expansive size of many rural states makes it very difficult, if not impossible, to consider charters as a viable school reform initiative. Consider the observations of Denise Juneau, Montana's superintendent of public instruction in 2010, who explained that her state had an average of one student per square mile and eighty-five districts with fewer than a hundred students. She further pointed out that all five of the most chronically low-performing schools in the state were on isolated, high-poverty American Indian reservations.[6]

In effect, the size of traditional public schools in rural states, and the immense distances between these schools, do not make charter schools a viable option for these states. This reality also exists in small school districts where small student enrollments negate the potential to advance charter schools. To further make this point, consider that in 2010 the National Charter School Research Project reported that "89 percent of U.S. school districts have no charter schools within their boundaries."[7] This is true in large measure because there are so many very small districts in the United States. The reality is that any potential for future charter school growth will be confined to large metropolitan areas, and will be focused on urban school districts.

Several additional concerns merit consideration in regard to the ability of charter schools, charter management organizations (CMOs), and charter school networks to scale up as quickly and as exponentially as charter school advocates might anticipate. Among these realistic concerns are

- The nation's fragile economy
- The credit crisis, which makes it difficult for CMOs and charter networks to secure needed funding
- The questionable long-term funding commitment of foundations and corporations
- The cost of renting or leasing additional classroom space

- The potential for escalating teacher and administrator salaries
- Dependence on local school boards' reducing local school budgets in support of further advancement of charter schools

Another important consideration relates to the ability of charters to recruit and retain a high-quality teaching staff. According to a 2010 research brief from the National Center on School Choice, "The odds of a charter school teacher leaving the profession versus staying in the same school were 130 times greater than those of a traditional public school."[8]

○ *Will charters play a major role in the "conversion" of low-performing schools?* Based on their present track record, charters have had very limited involvement in taking over low-performing schools and converting them into successful models of school improvement. This reality exists in spite of a strong plea by secretary of education Arne Duncan at the National Alliance of Public Charter Schools annual conference in 2009. In his speech, Duncan made a strong pitch to charter school leaders "to get involved in his push to 'turn around' 5,000 of the nation's lowest-performing schools."[9] At the same time, he promised that federal dollars would follow to support them.

It appears that the secretary's words fell on deaf ears, as it was reported in 2009 that "conversions" made up only about 10 percent of charter schools nationally. The 2009 Brown Center Report on American Education made the case that some of the largest charter management organizations were very reluctant to take on the responsibility of turning around failing schools. The report concludes that

CMOs "prefer starting schools from scratch rather than inheriting struggling schools." Possibly some of their reticence is attributable to the difficulty of undertaking such school turnaround projects, which is highlighted in the report: "It is fair to say, that the two cohorts of conversions in the present study evidence no significant institutional change in achievement over two decades."[10]

It appears that despite all of the ballyhoo the Obama administration continues to promote, representing charter schools as major players in the turnaround of low-performing schools, charter school leaders have remained on the sidelines as spectators—fully grasping the difficulty of exerting their energy as full participants in turnaround efforts. It appears that the administration has not taken into consideration the body of long-term research on school conversions, the findings of which clearly show few, if any, major changes in student achievement. Tom Loveless reinforces this point by noting a current study in which two cohorts of conversions were determined to have shown "no significant achievement over two decades."[11]

It is truly amazing that those attempting to legitimize the continued growth of charter schools as viable models for turning around low-performing schools have intensified their drumbeat, when it is blatantly obvious that charter providers have no appetite for taking on this challenge. Nor is there any validated research to support such an expansion. And yet, the beat goes on!

○ *What is the potential for closing low-performing charter schools?* It appears to be difficult to close charter schools that have a poor track record of improving student academic performance, or that have had serious issues relating to their fiscal management practices. I project that the "closure issue" will be magnified as states remove the caps on the number of charter schools allowed within their borders. This will probably lead to a rapid proliferation of new charter schools, which in many cases will result in multiple charter providers offering services in a given region. I predict that the focus on increasing charter schools will be predicated on a rush to quantity over quality—necessitating dramatically increased oversight by states and local school districts in regard to student achievement and fiscal management. It should be noted that the responsibility for such oversight will result in significant fiscal encumbrances for the states and school districts.

In a climate of rapidly expanding charter schools, I also project that inexperienced entrepreneurs will be attracted to the charter movement—and will subsequently rush onto the playing field with personal financial gain as a driving motivation in many cases. Such new players will have minimal if any experience in the operation of schools of any type, and will have little understanding of the complexities of teaching and student learning.

Gary Miron and Leigh Dingerson's "The Charter School Express" offers a sobering observation about the related implications for closing low-performing charter schools: "Whatever the factors, the growing body of independent research suggests that the combination of a rapidly expanding sector and the widely acknowledged challenge of actually closing charter schools once they have opened seem likely to cause a train wreck."[12]

Joe Nathan, a founder of the charter movement, offers a chilling and disturbing warning as to types of individuals and issues coming into play as the charter movement advances: "Some terrific charters are doing great things for kids, but charlatans have entered the field and have ripped off kids and taxpayers. Charter school organizations must develop better ways of screening out crooks and incompetents before they get to start schools."[13]

If closing low-performing and fiscally mismanaged charter schools is a problem today, it can be forecast that this issue will be magnified in the future in a climate of unrestricted expansion. For taxpayers and other funders providing the financial support for the growing number of charter schools, an old motto should give them pause: "Let the buyer beware!"

Charter school advocates' present love affair with charter schools is resulting in the diversion from traditional public schools of the time, energy, resources, and funding necessary to address the improvement of public education in a comprehensive and sustained manner. I believe that a holistic, long-term commitment to reforming traditional public schools would have the greatest impact on the greatest number of students.

Chapter Nine

GETTING CHARTER SCHOOLS BACK ON TRACK

As charter schools continue their advance into the school reform landscape, it is a fair and reasonable expectation that they should be held accountable for monitoring their progress in promoting student achievement, maintaining responsible and transparent financial operations, and employing equitable policies and practices in student admissions and retention.

Without question, there are a number of exemplary charter schools and charter school networks. These schools and networks should serve to inform other charters and traditional public schools (TPSs) in their pursuit of school improvement. Successful charter schools should also serve as models to be incorporated into a gradual and well-considered plan of expansion for new charter schools.

With this premise, the following recommendations are presented to provide a framework for addressing the common issues and concerns that continually frame the public discourse concerning charter schools and their potential for growth.

RECOMMENDATION 1: USE CHARTER SCHOOLS AS INCUBATORS

Charter schools that have, through validated evaluations, demonstrated improved student academic performance should share with TPSs the various teaching strategies, curriculum programs, instructional initiatives, and other approaches that have contributed to their success. Moving in this direction would serve to fulfill the initial vision of charter schools as incubators for new programs, policies, and strategies to improve student learning—which, in turn, could be replicated in TPSs.

Following a course of the type envisioned here would serve to forge a closer working relationship between charter schools and mainstream public education. It would also alleviate many of the concerns about charters as competitors; charters would instead be accepted as collaborators in working toward the mutually shared goal of improved student achievement.

If charter schools were used as incubators, the new and pioneering strategies in school reform undertaken therein would also serve to inform the policies and practices of new entrants into the charter school movement. According to the notion that "success breeds success," this would allow for a more gradual and research-based approach to the future growth of charter schools. Following a success-driven model of this type should quiet many of the charter schools' critics.

RECOMMENDATION 2: USE EVALUATION DATA RESPONSIBLY

It is incumbent on chief state school officers, school superintendents, and other state and district educational leaders to be fully conversant with the success stories of charter schools in their respective states. They should invest the time and effort to gain an understanding of the program, curriculum, and instructional components contributing to the success of these schools. They also need to be able to speak to factors that lead to low performance in other charter schools. Gaining such an understanding can advance their own planning in regard to how to replicate in TPSs the achievement strategies of the charter schools under review. In addition, in gaining this knowledge, they can better fulfill their leadership oversight responsibilities, providing support and as they consider granting approvals to new charter schools.

Regrettably, there is concern that state and local school district leaders may not, in fact, be aware of the successful charter schools residing in their own backyard. One of the lead researchers in the 2009 Center for Research on Education Outcomes (CREDO) study—widely recognized as the most comprehensive study of charter schools—later questioned the degree to which educational leaders had made efforts to fully comprehend the research on both successful and failing charter schools. To this point, the researcher added that the CREDO study "provided plenty to chew on but few educators took the bait." and the researcher also noted that "only a handful of states contacted the report's author for data that identified the schools, their respective locations, and their performance status.[1]

It is important to consider that the CREDO study identified both highly effective and low-performing charter schools in fifteen states and in Washington DC. This study presented a treasure trove of data to assess the status of an extensive number of charter schools—offering the potential to probe more deeply and analyze the conditions, programs, policies, and underlying strengths and weaknesses of the charters included in the study. State and school district leaders not affiliated with the study could have used the study's findings to educate themselves such that they might provide more informed oversight of the charter schools in their respective states.

All governing boards responsible for approving new charter schools must require that their leadership staff provide them with documented and validated charter school research findings prior to further expansion of charter schools. This logical method of operation encourages all of those charged with governing and approving charter schools to maximize the research and evaluation data employed in their ultimate decision making.

RECOMMENDATION 3: SEEK ACCOUNTABILITY FOR STUDENT ACHIEVEMENT AND FISCAL RESPONSIBILITY

It is vital to have accountability systems that allow charter schools to assess student achievement, exercise fiscal account-ability, and ensure fairness in student enrollment practices. This is a major consideration for publically funded charter schools—as opposed to privately funded charter schools—in that they are using taxpayer dollars to operate, thus necessitating that they be held accountable for the use of such funds.

Publically funded charter schools should also use the same basic accountability system that is employed to evaluate TPSs, ensuring a level playing field. The accountability system should include having charter school students take part in state-administered student tests, disaggregating all student data, ensuring accurate dropout and attrition numbers, providing enrollment numbers for all students with special needs and English language learners, and publically reporting all aggregate student results to parents and the general public. Operators of not-for-profit and for-profit charter schools should also embrace the accountability outline presented here, which would afford them greater credibility when comparing their school's results with those of TPSs.

It should also be standard operating procedure that whenever taxpayer dollars are used to support charter schools, public audits be conducted to monitor the use of such funds. Following this procedure would serve to protect the integrity of publically funded charters, and should be seen as a necessary step in guarding the public interest.

Often the argument presented by charter schools is that they require greater flexibility in carrying out their mission, thus dictating that they operate differently than TPSs in certain ways. Although one might concede this point, charter school advocates must clearly understand that with greater flexibility comes a need for greater accountability. These two concepts—flexibility and accountability—are reciprocal, with one being dependent on the other.

RECOMMENDATION 4: CLOSE
LOW-PERFORMING CHARTER SCHOOLS

The recent obsession of the charter school advocates has been to accelerate the growth of charters, with seemingly little concern for addressing the issue of school quality. I recommend that they confront this issue, and that they set in motion plans to close charter schools that are low performing, fiscally irresponsible, or both. Until the charter movement addresses this concern, it runs the risk of losing credibility with the general public and with corporate and foundation funders.

Margaret Raymond, director of CREDO, reinforces the need for the charter school proponents to accept this reality: "The issue of quality is the most important problem the charter school movement faces. The charter school movement works hard to remove barriers to charter school entry into the market . . . but now it needs to equally focus on removing the barriers to exit, which means closing under-performing schools." Raymond concludes with a succinct warning: "If the supporters of charter schools fail to address the quality challenge, they run the risk of having it addressed for them."[2]

It becomes incumbent on charter school authorizers to develop specific criteria to monitor and evaluate charter school performance over a reasonable period of time and, in turn, to put in place the mechanisms to close underperforming charter schools. The accountability measures outlined in Recommendation 3 should serve as a reasonable starting point for considering the relevant factors in evaluating charter school progress.

RECOMMENDATION 5: SLOW DOWN THE RAPID EXPANSION OF CHARTER SCHOOLS

Charter school advocates are adamant in their intentions to remove any and all state and school district barriers and caps preventing the advance of the growth of charters. This reality is evidenced by the dramatic expansion of charter schools over the past several years. However, such growth comes at a price, which charter school proponents must take into consideration—the most notable aspect of which is the issue of poor quality already cited. Placing the highest priority on opening new schools, without also continually seeking validated evidence of these schools' accomplishments, can ultimately hinder the long-term success of the charter school movement.

The importance of taking time and doing things right was a major consideration in Jim Collins's national bestseller *Good to Great*.[3] In this book, Collins presents his documented and researched review of what it takes for companies to move from good to great in their evolution. I would argue that the majority of Collins's findings are applicable to any organization, including charter schools, in the pursuit of success and development over time. Although by referencing the idea of "good to great" in conjunction with charter schools I do not mean to imply that they are approaching the level of organizational success Collins depicts, Collins presents a number of management and organizational tenets and cautionary considerations that are timely and relevant as the charter school movement advances.

Of particular importance is Collins's discussion of the "flywheel" and the "doom loop." Taken together, these two concepts offer an opportunity for charter school advocates to rethink their vision of accelerated growth. Decelerating the expansion of charter schools might mean that a higher premium is placed on quality and excellence. Collins initially presents the image of a huge, heavy metal disc called a flywheel, pointing out that it takes continuous effort, stamina, and commitment to task to eventually cause the flywheel to move forward with unstoppable momentum. He explains that "each turn of the flywheel builds upon work done earlier, compounding your investment of effort."[4]

The salient point in Collins's flywheel example should jump out to charter school advocates: "No matter how dramatic the end result, good to great transitions never took place in one fell swoop." Collins reminds the reader that successful organizational transformations do not take place "as if they jumped right through to breakthrough as some sort of an overnight metamorphosis."[5]

The salient message of the flywheel metaphor for charter school advocates is that it takes time to realize success, that there needs to be a resolution to stay the course, and that everyone supporting the movement needs to be energized for outcomes to be successful.

Enter Collins's doom loop, the implications of which should serve as a significant warning against the escalating growth of the charter school movement. In looking at companies that failed to show sustained growth and improvement over time, Collins concludes: "Instead of a quiet, deliberate approach of figuring out what needed to be done, and then simply doing it, the companies launched new programs—

often with great fanfare and hoopla aimed at 'motivating the troops'—only to see the programs fail to produce sustained results."[6]

Collins puts forth the premise that companies that did not improve wasted time and energy in "pushing the flywheel in one direction, stopping it, and then pushing it in another direction." He offers a concluding observation: "After years of lurching back and forth, the comparison companies failed to build sustained momentum and fell instead into what we came to call the 'doom loop.'"[7]

Charter school advocates, if they continue on their current course, may become victims of the doom loop. Consider the following doom loop examples that characterize charter school advocates, with their vociferous appetite for hastened charter school advancement:

- Demonstrating a continued obsession with "great fanfare and hoopla" in "motivating the troops" to promote growth initiatives, evident in the all-out push at the national and state levels.
- Not taking a deliberate and responsible approach to the launching of new charters, proceeding without any common vision, parameters, and boundaries. Secretary Duncan reinforces this point: "The charter school movement is putting itself at risk by allowing too many second- and third-rate schools to exist."[8]
- Not challenging inroads by new and inexperienced managers who are taking over charter schools, and who are pushing the flywheel in new and different directions.

- Not demanding that all charter school advocates have a unified vision for the future of the charter school movement.
- Not securing the commitment of all charter operators to pushing the flywheel in the same direction in pursuit of *quality*.

Taken collectively, the considerations just listed, unless addressed by charter school advocates, may very well constitute the doom loop for the future of the charter school movement. Charter school advocates can learn much from Collins's seminal work and its recommendations, which, if followed and implemented, may help the movement escape the doom loop and enhance its future potential.

A FINAL WORD

The future for charter schools will not be one of accelerated growth and celebrating the opening of new schools on a grand scale. The ultimate verdict on the future of charters will be rendered based on the degree to which they can demonstrate sustained growth in achievement over time, and on their fiscal responsibility in their use of taxpayer dollars. John Merrow offers a commonsense approach to the ongoing discourse on charter schools: *"Never forget that the name 'charter' on a schoolhouse door reveals no more about a school's quality than the word 'restaurant' tells you about the food."*[9]

Part Three

INTERNATIONAL COMPARISONS: HOW THEY SHOULD AND SHOULDN'T DRIVE REFORM

Chapter Ten

"OH, TO BE IN FINLAND!" A NEW LOOK AT THE PROGRAMME FOR INTERNATIONAL STUDENT ASSESSMENT

"Oh, to be in Finland!" is the continuing dirge of discontent sung by those who lament the standing of our nation's students in comparison with those of other countries. One would think they are interested in shipping everyone off to Finland for their K–12 education.

International comparisons of student academic progress are one of the key drivers of escalating school reform. The influence of comparing the academic progress of our nation's students with those of other developed countries cannot be minimized. In fact, in recent years we have witnessed the development of a "cottage industry" of researchers in this area, resulting in the issuance of numerous reports and articles—the majority of which bemoan the alleged low standing of America's students in contrast with students in other countries. Without question, such findings and assertions have captured the attention of the Obama administration, members of Congress, governors, state legislators, and corporate and foundation leaders, and others who see these comparisons as yet another opportunity to jump on the "bandwagon" of castigating public schools for their alleged shortcomings in international comparisons.

There has also been a lot of publicity surrounding the rankings of American students when compared to students from other countries. The news media's persuasive and compelling depiction of these often unfavorable comparisons has further fueled the intense debate over the quality of public education.

Taken in context, the broad and intensive coverage and criticisms of the supposedly low standing of America's students compared to their international counterparts have caused legislators and school reformers to call even more loudly for increased school improvement initiatives. The intensity of the drumbeat cannot be ignored in a book attempting to bring into clear focus the major, ill-advised attempts at school reform. In addition, I feel a responsibility to address the deficiencies and limitations of international comparisons—especially when these comparisons lie behind a number of misguided school improvement strategies.

Other important factors that will be reviewed in this chapter's discussion are the very different circumstances under which schools in other countries operate—and which set them apart from American public schools. These include differences in governance, staffing, funding, student enrollment policies, and social and economic conditions. Individually and collectively, these factors represent important considerations in assessing how well our students fare in relation to students in other countries.

It is also imperative to expose the myth underlying the purported relationship between our students' rankings on international comparisons and the short- and long-term economic prosperity of our nation. There is no question as to the importance of our nation's students' being academically prepared to compete in an international community and to contribute to our national welfare. However, to imply that how well our students score on one "fill-in-the-bubble" international test is an indicator of our nation's economic growth and stability represents a dead-wrong assumption. Continually placing the blame for the nation's economic shortfalls on the backs of students allows for a political sense of denial concerning the real problems underscoring economic realities. The enduring practice of "blame avoidance" also affords political and corporate leaders to shift the culpability for their own inability to improve our international economic standing to those who least deserve it—our nation's students and our system of public education.

PROGRAMME FOR INTERNATIONAL STUDENT ASSESSMENT

It is also important to address the major stimulus behind the discourse on international comparisons. Enter the Programme for International Student Assessment (PISA), which is the most highly recognized contributor to international student comparisons. This test is administered by the Organisation for Economic Co-operation and Development and measures pupils' skills in reading, numeracy, and science. The test is given as a common assessment of fifteen-year-olds across the globe every three years, as students complete what is, in many countries, their final year of compulsory education.

PISA test scores have without question become the leading international benchmark for tracking student progress. PISA scores and rankings essentially determine which of the participating countries will get to celebrate their high international standing, and which will have to despair over their low ranking. PISA results have served as a wake-up call for many countries—including the United States—and have led some to a "rush to judgment" concerning the causes of low student performance and, in turn, to develop often ill-advised school reform strategies. It should be noted that the United States has been the most aggressive in developing a mentality bordering on manic every three years, when the most recent PISA results are released.

I hope that this chapter will prompt the reader to review carefully the "hyped-up" international student comparisons and the role these assessments play in driving school reform initiatives. On such review, expectantly, *they will be dissuaded from considering a move to Finland*!

A New Look at PISA

To measure the scope and purpose of international comparisons and to debunk many of the erroneous conclusions reached by school reformers and corporate leaders concerning the PISA findings, it is necessary to examine what the test scores actually reveal.

Mark Twain once famously said: "There are three kinds of lies: lies, damned lies, and statistics." It seems appropriate to start this discussion with a reminder that the interpretation of statistical data is often contingent on the intent and interest (and at times even the biases) of the reviewer. It is also necessary to consider whether or not sufficient thought was given to the myriad factors influencing the results being examined. In fact, it can be posited that statistical reviews are often interpreted through the prism used by the reviewer. This background information on statistical interpretation merits careful reflection as we evaluate our international standing in regard to student academic performance.

In teasing out the meaning behind international rankings, it becomes important to highlight a number of contextual questions. Although the answers to these questions are difficult to glean from the PISA results, they would serve to further illuminate the complexities of international achievement comparisons. The questions that follow are pertinent to address in that it is very difficult to find answers to them in the PISA literature, they are absent from press releases, and they are buried in the reports or possibly have been ignored by the researchers.

- What is the total sample size of the student population being tested for whom results are reported, and what percentage of the age group being tested does it represent?
- Which schools and students are selected to participate, and after selection, which ones choose to participate?
- Which regions of the country are represented?
- Are vocational schools included?
- To what extent have children from low-income families dropped out of schools that were scheduled to take the PISA assessments before the test was administered?

- Are children with disabilities tested?
- Are students who speak a language different from the dominant language of the country in which they are tested included in the testing population?
- In summary, are all countries participating "on a level playing field"?

Other relevant factors that have an impact on the PISA results include the reality that students taking the test do so at different times, in different places, under different testing conditions, and under different proctoring protocols. If these cited factors are not enough to suggest the inherent inconsistencies in the administration of PISA, then consider a core discrepancy: the test takers take the reading test in different languages! Another factor, one that is consistently overlooked in international student comparisons (including PISA), is that the students participating in the assessments have no vested interest in the test results. In the United States, the results have no bearing on a student's classroom grades, class rank, high school graduation, or potential for college acceptance, and they have no influence on a student's entry into the workplace. America's students concentrate on those tests that have personal meaning for them, such as the SATs, the ACT, Advanced Placement tests, and International Baccalaureate examinations.

WHERE DO WE *REALLY* STAND?

Where, as a nation, do we stand on international comparisons? According to the most recent PISA results from 2011, the United States did better in some areas than other countries, but still not well enough.[1] Our reading score of 500 exceeded the global average of 493, for instance, but we were still academically dwarfed by Shanghai, China (526); Korea (539); Finland (536); Hong Kong, China (533); Singapore (526); Canada (524); and New Zealand (521). These scores once again gave the national media, legislative leaders, and policy wonks occasion to decry the sorry state of U.S. education. But wait; do these "average" scores provide a true illustration of our nation's standing?

Immediately following the release of the 2011 results, Mel Riddle, an associate director for high school services at the National Association of Secondary School Principals, personally conducted a careful and in-depth analysis of the results and offered an eye-opening view of what they mean. Riddle's initial and telling observation was that to assess the relative effectiveness of compulsory schooling, it is important to point out that PISA is only administered to those students who are enrolled in school. Riddle disclosed that according to his personal review of the 2008 Census Bureau data, the United States enrolls slightly more than 99 percent of the nation's fifteen-year-olds. By contrast, 95 percent of Chinese children enter school, but only 80 percent complete elementary school—with only 70 percent in poor, rural areas completing the first four grades of their system of education, which closely parallel the first four grades in the U.S. system of primary education. In other words, China's "random sample" of fifteen-year-olds is limited to a restricted number of students.[2] It seems obvious that any true and fair comparison of student assessment has to account for each nation's definition of "compulsory." Otherwise a circumstance exists whereby each participating nation is playing the "ratings game" by a different set of rules.

Those who continually lament the PISA rankings of U.S. students should actually take pride and comfort in the fact that 99 percent of our fifteen-year-olds are in school, and that as a nation we have responsibly passed the litmus test on randomization. The "lamenters" also need to consider the extent to which other participating nations may use different standards in obtaining their random sample. Until there is a common definition of "compulsory"—and an expectation that all nations will comply with the definition —U.S. students will continue to be at a disadvantage in the "ratings game."

THE ROLE OF POVERTY

We should also resist the alluring simplicity of a high average score. Although it's convenient to declare that one nation scores X points better than another, average scores often mask rather than illuminate the underlying reality. Unless the data are disaggregated, it is difficult to derive meaning from the results. When Riddle also took a look at American schools with varying degrees of poverty in contrast to schools in other developed countries, an interesting picture emerged. Schools in the United States in which 10 percent of students or less qualified for free or reduced-price lunch, a proxy for the poverty rate, produced students who scored an average of 551 on reading. This score is significantly higher than the average in Finland, which boasts a national poverty rate of less than 4 percent, and that is second only to Shanghai's. In fact, Riddle's research uncovered that when the data are adjusted for poverty, the U.S. outperforms every other country.[3]

It is disheartening to note that at the other end of the scale, a completely different picture surfaces. American students at schools with a population of 75 percent or more of students qualifying for free or reduced-price meals scored only 446. Riddle offered an intuitive concluding observation, playing off of an often-cited political quip: "When it comes to student achievement and school improvement, it's poverty, not stupid!"[4]

This broad set of data reminds us that U.S. schools do well by students who come to school ready to learn, but it is impossible to ignore the persistent correlation between poverty and performance—a relationship that continues to escape the critics of public education. They need to come to grips with the reality that students in poverty require intensive and continuous supports, and are confronted with conditions formal schooling alone cannot overcome. The critics must move away from their often ill-informed push for school reform initiatives, and instead concentrate their energy on addressing the all-inclusive needs of students living in poverty. History informs us that without addressing these attendant economic, societal health, and family support realities, it is extremely difficult to improve, on a large scale, the educational advancement of such students. There is no question that the education of this large cohort of children must be of paramount national concern.

Iris Rotberg, a researcher at George Washington University and a nationally recognized authority due to her comparative studies of education systems worldwide, informs us conclusively that the United States ranks high in two international competitions that we would prefer not to win: "We have one of the largest income and wealth gaps between rich and poor communities when compared with other industrial countries; and our system of school finance is also one of the most unfair."[5]

Rotberg also makes the salient point that the socioeconomic status of families is a significant problem in all countries, and that it accounts for about three-quarters of the variance in student performance across U.S. schools. She offers a dramatic conclusion that supports my earlier warning about the pervasive nature of poverty: "There is a myth that we can fix our schools without addressing the problems of poverty. We can't."[6]

Rotberg also references the implications of poverty for international comparisons: "A country with relatively high child poverty, but that encourages low-income children to stay in school, will be at a disadvantage in test score comparisons."[7] Although the United States may be at such a disadvantage, the moral resolve inherent in our national commitment to educating *all* children is its own reward. The critics need to grasp that unlike the majority of countries with which we are compared, we strive to ensure that *every* child receives a high-quality education. Such a commitment makes us proud as a nation, and should transcend any obsession others may have with international comparisons.

In summary, the fixation on international comparisons among those who place great significance on the PISA rankings, many of whom are not necessarily committed to addressing the underlying factors that have a negative impact on the educational advancement of our students, represents a major distraction—one that diverts time and attention away from tackling the problems confronting our students with the greatest needs.

DO INTERNATIONAL RANKINGS OF STUDENT ACHIEVEMENT PREDICT ECONOMIC GROWTH?

Pundits argue that our standing in the PISA results is an indicator of our nation's ability to compete in a global society. The simple logic they apply is that if other countries outperform us on international tests, it can then be expected that they will outperform us in the global marketplace. This point of view implies that one can forecast economic stability and growth based on the results of one test administered every three years—a rather absurd and illogical conclusion. If only it were so simple to predict the economic well-being of a country based on student test scores—if this were the case, the developers of PISA would probably have been considered for a Nobel Prize in Economics!

Once again, I cite Rotberg's extensive research, as it indicates the need for caution when making a connection between student test scores and economic prosperity. She concludes: "Test-score comparisons tell us little about the quality of education in any country . . . The fact that we can't interpret these test-score comparisons has not deterred us from concluding that a country's international competitiveness can be predicted from its ranking on international tests."[8]

In reality, there are several examples of nations that at one point had high levels of student achievement, and for which there was a related international expectation that their economic future was secured. Regrettably for these nations, however, such was not the case. To make this point, two specific examples follow.

The Russia Story

Russia, with the launch of Sputnik 1 in 1957, caused great clamor and consternation among members of the American public, the Eisenhower administration, and Congress, who were concerned that the scientific advances of what was then the Soviet Union put America's future in great peril. Of course, the immediate reaction was to place blame on our nation's public education system for falling behind that of the Russians. Articles and reports abounded that extolled Russia's educational prowess and condemned America's schools, teachers, and students.

Fast-forward to 1969, when America placed the first man on the moon, leaving Russia far behind in terms of accomplishments in space exploration. Ironically, no mention or credit for these accomplishments was ever given to the very same system of public education that only a few years earlier had been chastised for falling behind that of the Russians.

Also during the Sputnik era, the overhyped Russian educational system was projected to propel the country to new economic heights. Any rational person looking at Russia today—anyone reading a newspaper or listening to a news program—would be hard pressed to find evidence of any such attainment.

The Japan Story

The best example of false economic expectations based on student test scores can be traced to Japan. In the 1980s the Japanese system of education was extolled by the news media and the corporate sector as the driving force behind the nation's rapid and expanding economic growth. Its students excelled on tests and other measures of academic achievement. During this same period, not surprisingly, Americans disparaged U.S. schools as the source of the United States' own economic downturn. This was evidenced by extensive news coverage and various reports that lamented the condition of public education and its relationship to the economy. In fact, during that period of time there was a national "push" to promote the Japanese language in U.S. schools, with an expectation that our economic prosperity would be enhanced by our students' speaking Japanese. Fast-forward to 2012, and this front-page *Washington Post* article: "Japanese Firm Decrees 'Englishization.'"[9] The article notes the commitment of one Japanese executive to having his employees conduct all of their work in English. The article further explains that the Japanese CEO took this step in an effort to help his company expand and thrive in a shrinking domestic market. In addition, the Japanese company has recruited English-speaking people from around the world. This new and enlightened commitment to English has been in place for two years, and has spurred other Japanese companies to consider promoting English as the language of their workplace. There is a lesson to be taken from this "language awakening" in Japan—especially as it relates to the growing obsession with having more American students learn Chinese as a precursor to our nation's economic progress, a push fostered by the business community and evident in an increase in the number of schools offering more Chinese language courses. Perhaps we need to pause and reexamine our educational priorities.

The ultimate irony in the "Japanese success story" is that more than two decades later, although Japanese students continue to do well on tests, the Japanese economy has essentially imploded. For Japan and its stagnant economy, the 1990s have been referred to as the "lost decade."

In summary, the economic advancement of a nation does not directly relate to the number of questions students answer correctly on a test, or to a nation's brief spurt in educational attainment. The examples of Japan and Russia serve to make this point. Although education can be a significant factor, long-term economic growth and stability stem from a multitude of other factors. These include a nation's commitment to fervently pursuing and implementing sound economic policies and practices, and to providing the necessary national resources and funding to meet the needs of its people.

Howard Gardner, the distinguished professor at Harvard University, provides a lucid warning to those who insist on comparing U.S. students with those in other countries: "The goal of topping international comparisons is a foolish one, and the rush to raise one's rank is a fool's errand."[10] Rather than hitching our economic wagon to a future that many believe begins and ends with comparative test scores, we would be better served as a nation and as a society by heeding Gardner's noble exhortation: "Any country—and certainly one as prosperous and well positioned as the United States—should begin with a serious discussion of the kinds of human beings we would like to have and to be in the future."[11]

Enough said!

Chapter Eleven

A TRIP DOWN MEMORY LANE

The corporate and business community, the Obama administration, members of Congress, and policy wonks are unrelenting in their handwringing over whether public schools are inadequately preparing students for the workforce and thus undermining the American economy. But just as international student achievement tests are not predictors of economic decline or well-being, poor performance on such tests has little to do with our current economic woes.

Perhaps corporate leaders hope that by drumming up the "education crisis" they will distract the public from the catastrophic mortgage crisis, the greed of Wall Street, the credit card crunch, and the collapse of major financial institutions. All of these factors have resulted in billions of dollars in stock market losses, which in the opinion of many economists brought the United States to the brink of a depression. And perhaps they hope that the public will be too riled up by the "education crisis" to notice that some of these failing companies have shelled out millions of dollars in compensation to their chief executive officers. It is truly amazing that many these same corporate leaders have the audacity to promote performance pay for educators while—based on their payout enactments—they reward their own incompetence!

Paradoxically, and sadly, the strategy of shifting the blame has gained traction with the Obama administration and legislative leaders. Our national leaders should reconsider their position as they engage in the debate concerning the impact of public education on our nation's recent economic decline. They need to place the onus where it belongs, as vividly captured by the cover headline of the June 28, 2008, edition of *BusinessWeek*: "How Wall Street Ate the Economy."

A History of Misplaced Blame: Were We "a Nation at Risk"?

Erroneously placing blame on public schools for economic downturns is not a new development. Although the fixation on international student comparisons is gaining momentum in the press and among corporate leaders and policymakers, there is already a history of attempts to condemn public schools for other economic nosedives. It is important to point out that history also informs us that these earlier attempts were misguided.

Consider the 1990 report from the Commission on the Skills of the American Workforce, which stressed that skill development in schools was the major policy lever shaping the economy. "Flawed schools" had caused industrial productivity to "slow to a crawl," the report concluded, and "without radical school reform, a condition of permanently low wages could become a reality for the bottom 70% of all Americans."[1] Researchers Lawrence Mishel and Richard Rothstein have taken strong exception to these findings: "Events have proven this economic analysis was 'spectacularly' wrong. Within a few years of the 1990 report's publication, Americans' ability to master technological change generated an extraordinary leap in productivity. This acceleration, exceeding that of other advanced countries, was accomplished by the very same workforce that the Commission said imperiled our future." They further point out that in the period from 2003 to 2007, while wages of both high school– and college-educated workers stagnated, productivity grew by an extraordinary 11.5 percent.[2] It would seem that those who continually place the blame for our nation's economic stagnation on public education can learn valuable lessons from "spectacularly" flawed economic analyses of the past.

While we're going down memory lane, some readers may be experiencing a bit of déjà vu, revisiting memories of the now infamous *A Nation at Risk* report from 1983,[3] which warned that unless there was dramatic improvement in student achievement, Japan and Russia—because of their supposed superior education systems—would "eat our lunch." The reality is that the economies in Japan and Russia have been plummeting since the early 1990s—for almost twenty years—a decline that has been regularly and widely represented in the news media. During this same period— with the exception of the recession of 2007 to 2011, an event that can trace its roots to Wall Street greed and banking improprieties—the U.S. economy has flourished, and

U.S. productivity has increased. Not surprisingly, the critics of public education offered no accolades when the graduates of the same schools that *A Nation at Risk* decried were mastering modern technology and providing a solid foundation for continued economic growth. Today's prophets of gloom and despair need to be reminded that the Japanese and Russians did *not* "eat our lunch," and that they were in fact lucky to have "picked up our crumbs." (*A Nation at Risk* did, however, have some positive effects in driving school reform, which I'll get into in more detail in Chapter Fifteen.)

Educators across the country must remind the critics that public education, although an important contributor, is not the silver bullet for overcoming the demanding challenges of globalization and the other complex economic issues of our time.

THE INTERNATIONAL JOB MARKET

There have been numerous articles and various reports supporting the contention that American manufacturers are rushing to produce their goods and products in other countries—mainly China, India, Mexico, and Indonesia—often erroneously placing the blame at the doorsteps of public schools. In reality, the impetus for the outsourcing of jobs is that these countries provide their workers with minimal wages and health benefits, little job protection (such as union representation), and below-average working conditions. This exodus of employment opportunities for American workers is not in any way connected to the educational attainment levels of workers in these other countries. Simply stated, many of these other countries perform the work cheaper, and with less concern for the welfare of their workers.

Consider the reality that other countries often referenced as competitors (China, Russia, Japan, Mexico, and Germany, to name a few) do not even participate in the Programme for International Student Assessment (PISA) assessments. How, then, is it possible to use international comparisons of academic performance to depict these countries as competitors to the United States? To further expound on this unfair comparison, it was perplexing to read the headline of a recent *BBC Business News Periodical* article, "China: The World's Cleverest Country?," which offered the incredible conclusion that China's education system has been overtaking those in many Western countries. The article references the comments of Andreas Schleicher, a leader behind the highly influential PISA tests, who stated: "China's results in international education tests—which have never been published——are remarkable."[4] In effect, some level of testing was undertaken in China, but the results have never been revealed. An immediate question that needs to be addressed is, Why were these "remarkable" results never published? It would seem reasonable to expect that such results should be celebrated across the world.

Of course, as I referenced in the previous chapter, China has only 20 percent of its fifteen-year-olds still in school, representing a very small "random" sample of the country's population in comparison to America's 99 percent of fifteen-year-olds in school. This comparison represents a significant difference in sample size. Also, the only two Chinese regional provinces represented in the most recent PISA rankings were Shanghai and Hong Kong—and, as the article's author points out, "it was unclear whether Shanghai and another chart-topper, Hong Kong, were unrepresentative regional showcases."[5]

It is very troubling to digest Schleicher's additional statement: "In China, the idea is so deeply rooted that education is the key to mobility and success."[6] It seems that China's commitment to education as a "key to mobility and success" is confined to the top 20 percent of the country. It also appears obvious that its "deeply rooted" focus on education does not include social justice for its people. Perhaps rather than refer to China as the world's "cleverest country," we should interpret it as the "shrewdest" in covering up its unequal system of education.

The issue of jobs leaving America also became a contentious topic prior our participation in the 2012 Olympic Games in England, when it was uncovered that the uniforms to be worn by the U.S. Olympians were manufactured in China. This realization caused a maelstrom in the halls of Congress, with members expressing concern and anger that the uniforms were not produced in our own country. Although I could understand and appreciate the worries of our national leaders—and joined them in waving the flag of patriotism—they continued to avoid facing a stark reality: that it was simply much cheaper to manufacture the uniforms in China. In fact, as a front-page article in the *Washington Post* observed, the umbrage of Congress could have been extended to other manufacturers as well: "Congress has not yet suggested burning Spalding basketballs, Adidas leotards, Nike shoes or the Acer computers that the Olympic Committee will be using courtesy of their sponsors, all of whose products are manufactured abroad."[7]

My purpose in citing the Olympic uniform debacle is to stress the point that workers in the United States did not suddenly lack the ability to fabricate cloth and the ability to sew—nor had public education failed them. The simple conclusion to be drawn from the Olympic uniform fiasco is that the profit motive drove manufacturers and their stockholders to seek out the cheapest world markets in which to produce their goods and services.

It is grossly unfair to continue to chastise public schools for contributing to America's losing jobs abroad, when corporate greed should be identified as the real problem. America can stand tall and proud of its education system and the contributions to our economic growth and development it has made over the years. Do we still have issues to address in public education? Of course we do. We must address, the needs of students living in poverty nationwide, and we must demonstrate an unwavering commitment to confronting the many and diverse problems having an impact on large urban school districts.

Continuing to improve our system of public education and advance our economic prosperity has little to do with our rankings on international comparisons. Rather, it requires a national commitment to educational equity and excellence for all of our students. In turn, such a resolve will ensure the existence of future generations of Americans who will provide the imagination, resourcefulness, and innovative spirit to enhance our nation's economic future.

Chapter Twelve

GETTING INTERNATIONAL COMPARISONS BACK ON TRACK

Too much attention is given to international comparisons of academic achievement, with the assumption that these are indicative of a country's likelihood of success in a global economy. Rather, the time and energy devoted to dissecting such results and comparisons can be better spent following these recommendations:

RECOMMENDATION 1: UNDERSTAND AND RESPECT THE COMPLEX REALITIES OF INTERNATIONAL COMPARISONS

It is important to reflect on the influences that are having an impact on schools in different countries in different ways, and to gain an understanding of how these realities transfer to student assessment results. Examples of such influences include governance structures, instructional practices, student enrollment policies, methods of sampling student populations, and the allocation of funding.

RECOMMENDATION 2: ASSESS INTERNATIONAL COMPARISON RESULTS IN A MORE POSITIVE WAY

A comprehensive review of the data gleaned from results of international comparisons can contribute to building on the identified strengths of various countries and learning from each other's weaknesses. Such assessments should include reviews of curriculum offerings, pedagogical strategies, and student testing methodologies; class size considerations; and student grouping practices.

RECOMMENDATION 3: ANALYZE FACTORS THAT INFLUENCE INTERNATIONAL COMPARISONS

There exists a need to review and understand the various conditions, programs, and practices influencing the results of such international comparisons, to move toward a more international focus on successful school reform practices. This analysis should be undertaken within a climate of trust and sharing, with countries resolving to learn from one another as part of an international commitment to improve the education of all students in all countries—which should be a stated purpose of the Programme for International Student Assessment (PISA) assessments. In turn, American schools can gain further knowledge of successful educational programs and practices in other countries, which may have the potential for replication in our schools.

RECOMMENDATION 4: DETERMINE WHY U.S. REFORM STRATEGIES ARE "FOREIGN" TO OTHER COUNTRIES

It truly is ironic that the major reform strategies practiced in our nation's schools are not even considered by those countries (for example, Singapore and Finland) that are labeled as "top rated" on comparative assessments. School reformers in the United States need to come to understand why such initiatives as alternative schools (charters), standardized testing, school closures, alternative certification for teachers, standardized testing, and negative and pervasive incentives are "foreign" in other countries. Marc Tucker, author of an insightful paper on school reform, confirms this reality: "It turns out that neither the researchers whose work is reported on in this paper nor the analysis of the [Organisation for Economic Co-operation and Development] PISA data found any evidence that any country that leads the world's education performance league tables has gotten there by implementing any of the major agenda items that dominate the education reform agenda in the United States."[1]

We can also learn valuable lessons from the highly rated countries in regard to the high premium they place on teachers, as evidenced in teachers' preparation, induction, ongoing career development, competitive salaries, and elevated national stature.[2]

RECOMMENDATION 5: ALLOW FOR TEACHER AND PRINCIPAL INTERNATIONAL EXCHANGES

Through international exchanges, teachers and principals would conduct on-site reviews of the educational programs and practices of other countries. In particular, this would allow American educators to gain a more in-depth understanding of the teaching methods and leadership qualities of their international peers. I expect that teachers and principals from other countries would also benefit from observing our schools and classrooms.

RECOMMENDATION 6: CONVENE AN INTERNATIONAL CONFERENCE OF EDUCATORS

Bring together educators from countries that participate in the PISA assessments to discuss and assess the most recent PISA results, and to explore the factors contributing to the results of the high-scoring and low-scoring countries. An engaging face-to-face discourse of this type would serve to enlighten participants as to best practices in the other countries. Also, such a conference would generate a higher level of appreciation and support for international comparisons as sources of mutually beneficial information as opposed to the traditional classification of such assessments as being part of a "ratings game" among countries.

RECOMMENDATION 7: CONTINUE TO DEVELOP ONLINE CAPABILITIES

Improved online capabilities would enhance communication for educators from the participating countries, so that they may share information, strategies, and initiatives designed to advance student learning. Videos of classroom presentations should be an integral component of the online offerings.

A FINAL WORD

The potential exists for international comparisons to help educators and policymakers gain a greater awareness of the various educational programs, innovations, strategies, and instructional methodologies practiced in different countries. Such knowledge and awareness can be valuable assets in enhancing student achievement in all of the participating countries. In transitioning to this positive course, we must move away from using international assessments with international competition in mind.

If researchers continue to analyze comparative data, they must be diligent in taking into consideration the underlying educational platforms and social contexts of the participating countries. They must also have a realistic understanding of the limitations of using international rankings as a barometer to measure future economic growth and prosperity.

Part Four

THE FEDERAL ROLE IN SCHOOL REFORM: PROBLEMS AND SOLUTIONS

FEDERAL SCHOOL REFORM INITIATIVES: WHAT HAPPENED TO LOCAL CONTROL?

There is a significant contradiction inherent in the growing involvement of the federal government in school reform at the state and local levels, which is occurring against the backdrop of the highly decentralized system of public education. This contradiction is embedded in four major realities:

1. *The Tenth Amendment to the U.S. Constitution clearly states, "The powers not delegated to the United States by the Constitution, nor prohibited by it to the States, are reserved to the States respectively, or to the people."* Nowhere in our Constitution is the federal government delegated the power to regulate or oversee public education. The reality is that the constitutional authority for our nation's schools resides with the states, which in turn have delegated this responsibility to local school boards—which represent a uniquely American tradition of local control.

2. *The imperative of local control is part of a long-standing American tradition, one that is embedded in the nation's psyche and carries out the vision of our founding fathers.* Consider Thomas Jefferson's exhortation during our nation's infancy, "The control of our nation's schools should be lodged in the ward."[1] He refers here to something akin to what we now call local control, sending forth a clear message as to expectations for control of public education. Thus, there are approximately 14,500 school boards across the nation, which have been entrusted by their respective states with the responsibility and authority to provide free public education in their school districts. In effect, the states have passed on to school boards their constitutional requirement to provide access to quality education and to promote equal educational opportunity for all students.

3. *The federal government provides only 9 to 10 percent of the nation's total funding for its public system of K–12 education.* The states and local communities contribute the remaining 90 percent of public school funding— funding that is supplied by local citizens, in the form of the tax burden they must assume to meet this obligation. There exists in this case a real conundrum in interpreting the alternative "golden rule"—"He who has the gold makes the rules." In effect, in applying this rule, the federal government should have minimal standing in driving a national education reform agenda, particularly when it has such a minuscule commitment to funding public education. It seems a real mystery why governors, chief state school officers, educators, and school boards are so passive in allowing the federal

government to dictate the terms and conditions of school reform at the state and local school district levels. To continue down this path is a significant distortion of the golden rule, and it allows the player with the least commitment to dictate the game plan for those who have made a substantial state and local funding commitment.

4. *The United States does not have a centralized system of public education, unlike many other countries to which we are often compared.* Consider the reality that we do not have a national curriculum, and minimal power is entrusted to our U.S. Department of Education and its secretary of education——although the department and the secretary do, at times, act as though they have a sense of omnipotence in driving school reform. Dan Domenich, executive director of the American Association of School Administrators, has, on several occasions, emphatically noted that the secretary of education cannot be the superintendent of 14,500 school districts!

In summary, the federal government has played by its own set of rules in driving a national school reform agenda by completely disregarding the purpose and intent of the Tenth Amendment to our Constitution, pushing aside the inherent rights of states and local school boards, and displaying a lack of concern about the miniscule amount of funding it provides when compared to the major tax burden incurred by citizens in support of their local schools. This is evidenced by the mandates and onerous burdens imposed on states, schools districts, and schools without any consideration for state and local input. Such burdens and mandates are implicit in the No Child left Behind (NCLB) legislation and the federally driven Race to the Top and School Improvement Grants initiatives.

In this context, is it any wonder that there is a growing sense of frustration and "pushback" in states and in local school districts concerning the escalating role of the federal government in school reform? In effect, the sense in our nation's schools is that reform initiatives are "being done to us rather than with us"! This sense of disavowal is succinctly captured by an Alexis de Tocqueville quote: "It's in the democratic citizen's nature to be like a leaf that doesn't believe in the tree that it is a part of."[2]

This quote suggests that citizens naturally distrust the larger systems of government that have an impact on their lives. In turn, imagine the heightened level of distrust local school boards and school districts experience when confronted with the continued intrusion of federal educational mandates and burdensome intervention strategies. School reform can only take place in a climate of trust, cooperation, and shared commitment among all of the parties involved— a climate that does not exist now among our government leaders and members of the education community.

NCLB: THE LAW OF THE LAND

Why focus on NCLB in a new book on school reform? Isn't it old news? On the contrary, NCLB is alive and kicking: consider the reality that until the U.S. Congress votes to abandon or modify the existing law, it does not "sunset." In effect, it remains the "law of the land." NCLB also represents an important intrusion of the federal government into local control of education and deserves examination here.

NCLB is nothing less than an egregious example of illogical and divisive legislation that has been imposed on educators, school boards, and municipalities by the federal government since its inception in 2002. Consider that responsibility for the actual development of NCLB was given to a select few White House policy analysts in the Bush administration, and to members of the late senator Edward Kennedy's staff. There may have been some minimal representation from certain other congressional offices, but ironically there were no educators involved in the process. In fact, the input of Rod Paige, the secretary of education at that time, was conspicuously absent from the NCLB deliberations. In effect, those individuals who crafted the new legislation had very little if any knowledge of the many and complex responsibilities of teachers and school administrators; child growth and development; the nature of human variability; the problems with relying on standardized testing as a sole assessment measure; the debilitating impact of poverty on students; and the unrealistic set of expectations, for example, embedded in the legislation's requirement that all children be proficient in 2014. Later, I refer to this unrealistic expectation as a "Lake Woebegone" effect placed on schools, students, and educators. Operating with such knowledge deficiencies did a disservice to members of the education community, parents, and school board members, and from day one of the implementation of NCLB, these same individuals who were the "victims" of this mandate have grasped the meaning of what it feels like to be a "leaf" that no longer believes in the "tree" of which it thought it was a part!

Compounding the ultimate passing of NCLB was a strong belief within the education community and among state and school district leaders that a significant majority of Congress had taken the time neither to read nor to fully digest the voluminous legislative tome put before them in an abbreviated period of time—generally referenced as an "overnight" exercise, possibly implying no more than two to three days for review. Over the ten years since the passage of NCLB, many legislators have admitted that they simply did not, at the time, give this significant legislation a fair and comprehensive review prior to casting their vote. Of course, I would agree that those who crafted the law were well intentioned, and that their efforts did in fact produce several important components of meaningful school reform, including a strong commitment to revealing the great disparities in educational outcomes for various subgroups of a school's population; stressing the importance of accountability in student achievement; disaggregating achievement data, thereby exposing the inadequacies of what are represented as "average" school scores in determining student progress; requiring that parents receive comprehensive and timely reports on their child's school progress; and elevating the level of parent and community consciousness, resulting in a greater resolve to support our nation's public schools.

An Unprecedented Shift in the Federal Role

NCLB represented a major and unprecedented shift in the federal role in public education, departing significantly from prior federal education legislation, including the Elementary and Secondary Education Act in 1965, the Disabilities Act in 1978, and the reauthorized Improving America's Schools Act in 1994. These acts represented federal education policy targeted at equalizing educational opportunity for all students, and at redistributing financial resources to students with the greatest needs. The funding for these programs was largely formula driven, and the acts put in place regulations for the use of the funds. But these earlier federal initiatives differed from NCLB in that they made no attempt to mandate specific programs or strategies as a condition for receiving federal funding. NCLB marked a sea change in the expansion of federal authority in public education, representing a greater intrusion into programmatic decisions, which had historically been made at the local level. For example, NCLB set specific timelines for results, identified failing schools, and imposed sanctions for noncompliance. In addition, the framers of NCLB seemingly placed the greatest burden on the public schools as the sole determinant of equity in educational outcomes, the nation's economic prosperity, and closing the achievement gap. The framers of NCLB gave minimal consideration to the societal environments within which public schools operate, the significant impact of poverty on children and families, and the major disparities in wealth distribution in America. I would posit that NCLB has, as what one hopes is an unintended consequence, served to portray public education in a continuing negative spotlight. Harvey Kantor and Robert Lowe offer the following pronouncement, which reinforces my contention: "NCLB suggests that low achievement will improve if students, teachers, and schools work harder. While this rhetoric may suggest a greater focus on equal education opportunity, it allows policy-makers to make education the sole social and economic policy."[3]

Where Did NCLB Come From?

Seminal questions that need to be asked to further understand this legislation are

- Where did the motivation for NCLB come from?
- Who were its original champions?
- On what body of research is it based?

The answers are interesting, pointing out the extreme flaws inherent in NCLB's development and implementation. NCLB was predicated on the so-called "Texas miracle" —the alleged academic successes of the Houston Independent School District in Texas. In his inaugural year as president, George W. Bush extolled the track record of Texas schools, and the leadership of Houston superintendent of schools Rod Paige—who would later be named the U.S. secretary of education. President Bush and members of his staff envisioned and aggressively promoted the "Texas miracle" as the bedrock on which the federal government should build public school reform. The irony is that after NCLB was enacted, numerous reports and articles brought into serious question the successes of Texas schools, citing highly inflated school completion rates and a major disparity between the high rates of success on the state-administered proficiency test and the state's very low scores on the National Assessment of Educational Progress (NAEP)—which is considered the nation's report card on academic achievement. In effect, there was no viable body of research or any evaluation to support the claims based on which NCLB was "sold" to Congress, educators, and the general public. The ultimate irony is that in the NCLB legislation, the term *scientifically based research* is used 125 times to describe the requirements to which districts and schools should adhere when implementing school reform strategies. With such a commitment to research, those responsible for crafting NCLB should have done their own homework prior to advancing legislation for which there was no valid documentation to justify its imposition on our nation's schools.

IS PROFICIENCY FOR ALL STUDENTS POSSIBLE OR EVEN DESIRABLE?

One of the initial shortcomings of NCLB was its unwavering and misguided commitment to academic proficiency for all students by 2014. This goal is as absurd as considering the following expectations to be met by 2014: all golfers will shoot par, all citizens will play the piano, all citizens will vote, and all students will graduate from college. These are indeed lofty and desirable goals, but unrealistic to achieve.

Yet Congress and President Bush were unfazed by the use of the word "all" when it pertained to student proficiency by 2014. NCLB codified this goal in 2002, and educators have been scrambling to achieve it ever since. Allowing each state to have its own definition of proficiency based on standards that vary widely from state to state compounds the absurdity—made even greater by the expectation that all students will pass proficiency tests by some arbitrary point in time, the magical year 2014.

"Proficiency for all" has been termed an oxymoron by Richard Rothstein and his colleagues at the Economic Policy Institute. They argue that "no goal can simultaneously be challenging to, and achievable by, all students across the entire achievement distribution." They further note:

> There is no aspect of human performance or behavior that is not achieved in different degrees by individuals in a large population.
>
> If we define "proficiency for all" as the minimum standard, it cannot possibly be challenging for most students. In turn, if we define "proficiency for all" as a challenging standard (as does NCLB), the "inevitable" patterns of individual variability dictate that significant numbers of students will still fail—even if everyone improves. So whether we're measuring performance in golf, piano, or academics, some performers will be more successful than others—or it's not a standard worth setting. The word "all" as used in NCLB, then, is simply not achievable, and it defies the reality of human variability.[4]

Harold Howe II, former U.S. commissioner of education during the 1988 NAEP reauthorization process, noted the importance of respecting human variability in assessing student outcomes in another testing context. He offered the following insight as Congress was then attempting to identify achievement goals for each age and grade in the

NAEP subject areas: "Most educators are aware that any group of children of a particular age or grade will vary widely in their learning for a whole host of reasons. To suggest that there are particular learnings or skill levels that should be developed to certain defined points by a particular age or grade is like saying all 9th graders should score at or above the 9th grade level on a standardized test. It defies reality."[5]

But, the fallacy of universal proficiency aside, we must acknowledge that using a proficiency level as the sole standard for student achievement makes for a hollow victory statement. Most proficiency tests are based on very low standards—reflecting the attainment of basic reading and math skills. Where is the commitment to higher standards in these subject areas? Where is the commitment to giving students a greater scope of knowledge, including in the arts, humanities, and sciences; in physical education; and in health? How does a goal of low-level proficiency prepare students to thrive in an expanding global society that demands creativity, imagination, and ingenuity?

Alas, as long as we keep the bar low and are content with basic skills attainment as a measure of success, we are truly doing a disservice to all students—particularly students from low-income families and minority students. As I recently heard one educator observe, "We teach the basics to students from lower socioeconomic backgrounds. We teach knowledge to affluent students."

NCLB's proficiency mandates reveal a fundamental lack of understanding of what "proficiency" means and how it should be measured. Yet we are likely to persist in the proficiency fallacy through 2014—and possibly in the future—and continue to determine how well a student is achieving based on one test administered at one time each year. In reality, we know that true assessments of student performance must be based on multiple criteria that are considered in the daily observations and evaluations of classroom teachers. Their assessments are not snapshots of student performance. Rather, they take place on a daily, hourly, and often minute-by-minute basis. Student learning is a journey over time, and therefore should be carefully assessed over time. There are no effective shortcuts for measuring proficiency—only convenient ones. And if the federal government persists in its involvement in education, it must understand the difference.

The federal government also needs to be cognizant of, and concerned by, the reality that a student can be proficient in one state and not proficient in another. This outcome is based on the fact that the NCLB legislation, as was noted earlier, allows each state to set its own bar for determining proficiency. It will be interesting to see how members of Congress will explain to parents in their respective states that the degree to which a child is achieving academic proficiency is confined to their state alone, and that the child's academic standing may change dramatically by simply crossing a state line.

One would expect that the framers of the legislation and the members of Congress who supported it would be hard pressed in the year 2014 to explain a system that has resulted in such disparities. This is a problem that needs to be immediately addressed, or else in 2014 there will potentially be fifty ships of state arriving at Lake Woebegone, sailing under false colors of academic achievement.

The Testing Problem: There Is No Single Best Answer

Moving on to another negative impact of NCLB, public education is presently immersed in "accountability madness," relying on simplistic assessment models that largely measure basic skills and that have resulted in a bonanza of off-the-shelf multiple choice assessments. As Daniel Pink, author of *A Whole New Mind*, has cogently noted: "If the global supply chain ever encountered a shortage of No. 2 pencils, the American education system might collapse."[6]

Educators strive to endow students with a full breadth of knowledge and to teach them to critically select and apply that knowledge to solve complex problems, yet multiple choice questions assess them very narrowly on their ability to "fill in the oval—completely." Such assessment models do not account for students' different learning styles, the context of their learning, and the ambiguity of many test questions.

When we instruct students to "select the best answer," we presume all minds think alike (all brains are functioning in the same way). As shown in the following examples—many of which have been humorously used in various presentations over the years—a group of first graders was asked to complete a set of well-known proverbs. Consider if our "best" answers are any better than theirs:

- Strike while the . . . bug is close.
- Don't bite the hand . . . that looks dirty.
- A bird in the hand . . . is going to poop on you.
- Better late than . . . pregnant.

Are these students wrong? No!

Such unconventional thinking is not unique to students at the elementary level. Examples abound at the secondary level as well:

Teacher: "What is the capital of Italy?"
Student: "I."

Is the student wrong? No!

Teacher: "Explain the shape of the graph."
Student: "It's curvy, with a higher bit at the end
             and a rather aesthetically pleasing slope
             downward toward a pretty flat straight
             bit. The actual graph itself consists of
             two straight lines meeting at the lower
             left-hand corner of the graph and
             moving away at a 90-degree angle. Each
             line has an arrowhead on the end."

Is the student wrong? No!

In each of these examples, students have provided answers that have meaning for them. By conventional bubble-test rules, they would receive precisely no credit because their answers do not conform to a test publisher's "one-size-fits-all" responses, and they do not enable the enforcers of NCLB to gather uniform accountability data.

It seems that the framers of NCLB—in their unwavering obsession with holding schools accountable based on a constricted view of student achievement—have little, if any, understanding of how children learn, and a lack of knowledge concerning the variability of their learning styles. It would have indeed served a meaningful purpose had the NCLB framers taken a basic course in brain research prior to imposing their dysfunctional system of accountability on our nation's teachers and students. In his book *Brain Rules,* John Medina offers a strong warning that legislators and federal officials obviously did not heed in their zealous rush to accountability:

> You cannot change the fact that the human brain is individually wired. Every student's brain, every customer's brain is wired differently. That's the Brain Rule. You can either accede to it or ignore it. The current system of education chooses the latter, to our detriment.[7]

It also seems obvious that the policy gurus and legislators promoting school reform through NCLB had no knowledge of Howard Gardner's seminal work on multiple intelligences, in which he emphatically notes that "people do learn, represent and utilize knowledge in many different ways." He continues: "These differences challenge an educational system that assumes that everyone can learn the same material, in the same way, and that a universal measure is sufficient to test student learning."[8]

It should not, then, come as a surprise that educators are so turned off by the NCLB accountability mandates, which emphasize one single test, evaluate schools by examining a narrow cross-section of the curriculum, and distort what teachers teach and students learn.

Ironically, NCLB, which was aimed at creating a more equitable system, may actually have produced greater inequity through its heavy focus on testing. Successful schooling is now reduced to addressing only proficiency in math and reading. In effect, the school curriculum has been highly distorted and constricted. This myopic focus has had significant consequences, including the continual transferring of school personnel and resources to mathematics and reading at the expense of the arts, civics, health, and physical education, as well as a distraction from addressing the emotional and social well-being of students.

Furthermore, it's unrealistic to assess student achievement and hold schools accountable based on such a constricted curriculum. The "reformers" of public education don't seem to get that it's lunacy to ignore what takes place in classrooms on the other 175 days when the state assessment is not being administered. It appears that to them, the brain is only relevant on test day. They don't get that schools have a primary responsibility to educate children for life.

And they don't get that writing a poem, singing a song, dancing a dance, participating in a drama club, engaging in physical education, understanding civics and democracy, and becoming aware of social and moral obligations are all part of the daily responsibilities of students in every school. John Ciardi, a distinguished poet, once captured the importance of the arts: "An ulcer is an unkissed imagination taking out its wrath for having been gilted—the undanced dance, the unwritten poem, the unsung song, the unpainted watercolor . . ."[9] One should ask, How many students in our schools today have experienced an "unkissed imagination" due to the narrow-minded focus of those who just don't get it? Classes in the arts, the humanities, civics, health, and physical education are essential learning experiences—but, alas, NCLB advocates have little time for them in the "assessment" of public education.

Taking into account the significant issues raised in this chapter concerning NCLB, I would argue that this legislation alone represents one viable reason why the federal role in public education is highly suspect, that it moves us away from meaningful and comprehensive reform, and that it has fostered a climate of distrust among those responsible for its implementation—our nation's educators.

Chapter Fourteen

RACE TO THE TOP AND SCHOOL IMPROVEMENT GRANTS: HELPING SCHOOLS OR HOLDING THEM HOSTAGE?

The race to the Top (RTT) and the School Improvement Grants (SIG) initiatives have provoked frustration and pushback in school districts across the country—an outcome that has been widely referenced in the news media and has resulted in a vocal chorus of dissent from educators.

RACE TO THE TOP

Consider that the RTT initiative provided billions of federal dollars to states through a grant competition. The successful winning states had to agree to put in place specific federally mandated reform strategies, the most notable of which were promoting greater accountability for teachers (including merit pay considerations); changing state laws to allow for dramatic increases in the number of charter schools; and placing a greater emphasis on changing state laws pertaining to teacher tenure and the terms and conditions of teacher contracts. In effect, states pursuing these grants were being held captive to federal models of reform for which there was a very small if any research base, and which arguably emanated from a sense of entitlement by the U.S. Department of Education (ED) in setting its own agenda for school improvement. If federal officials thought that the large number of states entering the competition was evidence of the validity of the ED reform models, they were missing something important—based on my numerous conversations with state and local education leaders, it seems that most state officials saw the competition as a race to the money, not to the top!

In fact, as this chapter is being written, numerous reports and newspaper articles have concluded that a large number of funded states are well behind in keeping the "reform promises" that were embedded in their original applications. In an attempt to rectify this reality—and to address the backlash from state leaders, educators, and the general public—the ED agreed to waive certain requirements of RTT. The ED only granted waivers based on its own terms and conditions, thus not allowing states to determine their own specific waiver needs. Again, this represents a classic example of federal officials thinking that they know more about local reform needs than do the states that have the constitutional authority over the education of their residents, and more than the educators working in the vineyard of public education.

SCHOOL IMPROVEMENT GRANTS PROGRAM

Perhaps the most egregious federal edict is embedded in the infamous four turnaround models, which are the underpinnings of the SIG program.

As a reminder, let's take a look at the four distinct models of the SIG program, from which school districts must make one choice when considering the fate of a school or its faculty:

- *Turnaround.* The principal and half of the faculty are replaced. The new principal gets megaflexibility.
- *Restart.* The school is closed and reopened as a charter or under new for-profit management. The principal is replaced.
- *Closure.* The school is closed, and students go elsewhere. The principal, along with everyone else, is dismissed.
- *Transformation.* Steps are taken to transform the school's culture and implement a rigorous performance-based evaluation system. Students and teachers receive more support, and leadership teams are granted more flexibility. But first, the principal is replaced.

I applaud the ED's commitment to turning around the nation's lowest-performing schools, and this point merits repeating. It is also not my intention to defend substandard principals. It might be true that the principals in some of these lowest-performing schools are the agents of stagnation who have to go before real progress can commence. Or perhaps, and very likely, the low performance results from a combination of factors and inadequate leadership at various levels. What's frustrating is that the ED has displayed no real interest in even entertaining the possibility that the principal is not at the heart of the problem. The implied message is: whenever a school is struggling, the school principal is the problem and must be replaced.

It is difficult to understand the logic that puts in place a plan to replace principals as the first course of action— even before any attempt is made to identify the cause of the problem. It seems that the ED has not considered that dismissing one leader without holding other leaders in the school district accountable might create a new problem while failing to identify the old one.

Despite its earnest commitment to a worthy goal of turning around the nation's lowest-performing schools, the Obama administration has proceeded with models of improvement that are untested; raise angst, despair, and frustration among educators; and will ultimately cause havoc among parents and within communities. And it seems unlikely that these SIG turnaround models will improve much of anything. It has been very difficult to find a body of validated research to support the imposition of any of the models proposed because, to paraphrase secretary of education Arne Duncan, waiting for research results slows down the process of school reform—a pronouncement that has given whiplash to educators who have been laboring under the "scientifically based research" doctrine of No Child Left Behind (NCLB) for the past decade.[1] Granted, the previous administration's appreciation of real research was—to be kind—fluid. But to completely abandon the use of research and drive decisions instead based on policymakers' intuition will ultimately do more harm than good.

What Does It Really Take to Turn Around a School?

There's a wide body of research that indicates it generally takes three to five years to turn around a low-performing school. This is very evident in the success of the Breakthrough Schools (BTS) initiative—a program sponsored by the National Association of Secondary School Principals (NASSP). During my tenure at the NASSP, we were proud to recognize, on an annual basis, Breakthrough Schools— schools that against all odds and with many of the same characteristics of failing schools achieved great success in advancing student progress. The BTS program's ability to identify successful schools can be attributed to several factors, one major factor being the extensive time required for a turnaround. And given that the great majority of BTS principals had been in place at least four years (with a minimal turnover of faculty as well), it's disturbing to realize that had these four SIG models been in place during their tenure, some of these principals probably would not have survived long enough to see the school succeed.

The importance of adequate time and the need for continuity of staff and programs apparently have been lost on federal officials, who continue to insist that a principal must be replaced if he or she has been in a failing school for at least two years. Based on strong backlash from educators and parents, the ED changed its stance and allowed principals with three years of experience in a failing school to remain in their position, even if the school has been failing for two years or more.

By contrast, the Obama administration's notion of success is best illustrated by events in Central Falls, Rhode Island, in February 2010, when the entire high school faculty and administration showed up one day to find pink slips in their boxes. President Obama himself praised the move, but with a caveat: "If a school is struggling, we have to work with the principal and the teachers to find a solution. We've got to give them a chance to make meaningful improvements."[2] A bit of fact checking reveals the ironic detail that the principal who was set to be terminated was the school's sixth principal in seven years, in place only since September 2008—so probably not a factor in the school's persistent low performance. The greater irony is that the president's tempered sentiments are not reflected in the turnaround models, which all call for termination first, then working with the staff.

What Does It Take to Replace Staff and Faculty?

Central Falls was just an initial example of the turnaround policies in practice. Now that billions of dollars are flowing to states to execute the four turnaround models, the same scenario may very well be repeated a couple thousand times. So before we sink too much money into random chances for success, the administration has a responsibility to address a few questions, considering that all models call for replacing the principal and some call for replacing at least half of the faculty. For one thing, where will we find so many high-quality replacements? The Obama administration aims to turn around the nation's five thousand lowest-performing schools according to these models, so we'll need to find five thousand new principals and tens of thousands of new teachers. Memo to district officials: "You know those legions of highly competent educators you've been keeping in reserve all these years? This would be a good time to unleash them."

Researchers at Johns Hopkins University note that one-fifth of the nation's two thousand high school "dropout factories" are in rural areas with small populations. What accommodation can be made to help these schools find new staff members? It is, to quote Yogi Berra, déjà vu all over again. NCLB created mayhem in rural schools with its "highly qualified teacher" ruckus, which completely ignored the reality in which rural schools exist. Simply, schools in remote areas with small populations face particular challenges in attracting competent educators. Yet even these schools will be expected to find new leaders and new teachers or, in the event of closure, to transport students who might already spend more than two hours a day on a bus even greater distances to another school.

Other questions persist:

- How is a district to summarily replace staff if they are contractually employed and their most recent evaluations rank them as satisfactory or superior? Issues of fairness, seniority, and due process are continuing to impose a burden on districts, which may have to address accusations of unfair labor practices. In this scenario, energy and resources are being or will be redirected from school improvement to legal proceedings.

- Does any valid research exist to attest to the quality of the replacement teachers, and how long their tenure will be in these schools? It would appear that the verdict is out on this important question, and yet the Obama administration continues to promote the egregious policy of forcing the replacement of principals and teachers as a focus of school reform.

- How will the Obama administration deal with the potentially disproportionate impact of the turnaround models, over time, on minority educators? This is a significant issue in that urban low-performing schools are staffed largely by minority educators. Are there enough minority teachers and principals available to replace those who are terminated or transferred?

A number of the models call for educators to be "replaced" and reassigned to other schools, presumably because their incompetence contributed to the school's low performance. If they are incompetent, how can the administration justify their reassignment to another school? The reality is that since the SIG program's inception, the vast majority of principals and teachers forced to leave their "failing schools" have simply been reassigned to other schools in their respective districts. This outcome speaks clearly to the inadequacy of the law, which enables transferring staff within a district as opposed to weeding out incompetence. In addition, the practice of "transferring the problem" has let superintendents and school board members off the hook in terms of making difficult personnel decisions and avoiding potentially costly litigation.

What Happens When the SIG Money Goes Away?

Another significant concern, which the Obama administration should contemplate, is the reality that many of the "turnaround schools" have received substantial federal financial assistance to facilitate their improvement. If the money becomes one of the significant determining factors in the improvement of a school, it will be very difficult to sustain the school's progress, or to replicate the successful initiative in other schools. This outcome will be probable unless there is a commitment to infusing new federal fiscal resources into schools. To vividly make this point, I met a high school principal in New Mexico whose school had received a $3 million SIG grant over three years. Even if the school shows improvement at the end of the three-year period, will the school be able to sustain its improvement when it loses its annual subsidy of $1 million? In addition, will whatever successes are realized be transferable to another high school without a new stream of federal money? In effect, the much-heralded SIG initiative may ultimately celebrate "victory gardens" when what is needed is an "amber waves of grain" approach to school reform.

Congress should take great pause prior to any future funding of initiatives that emulate a SIG program. Rather, should new funds be available to support school reform, it would serve a much greater end if the new monies were more widely distributed directly to states and school districts to reach a larger number of schools. There will also be a greater potential for replication of successful models and school-based accountability if states and school districts develop and implement their own intervention strategies. Consider that educators have a greater understanding, as professionals, of the underlying issues influencing student performance; are conversant with their respective parent bodies; and will be more likely to buy into reform strategies into which they have had significant input.

Secretary Duncan has often referenced, in his many speeches, a belief that when a school continues to perform in the bottom 5 percent, something dramatic needs to be done. This simple statement reveals at the same time the Obama administration's fundamental philosophy of school improvement and its inherent lack of understanding about what school improvement really requires. I fully agree that we need to see dramatic improvement, but such improvement does not necessarily result from dramatic action! There is no simple, sexy, silver-bullet "dramatic" fix for persistent low performance. As we've been repeatedly reminded by schools that have turned themselves around, what's necessary is pretty bland, totally unsexy, boring, undramatic, time consuming, and slow to progress. It requires digging into data, crunching numbers, and discovering deficiencies; then identifying, implementing, and measuring the effect of appropriate interventions. And then it has to be done all over again. Inconveniently for the Obama administration, you can't reduce school reform to a sound bite, and you won't see results overnight. And given the challenging contexts in which these low-performing schools function, it's unreasonable for the Obama administration to simply presume that the educators who work in low-performing schools have been unwilling to provide, or are incapable of providing, high-quality education to their students— without first offering them the scaffolding to prove otherwise.

The indiscriminate SIG shake-up models have ensured only one thing: that these schools have been shaken up! But such a shake-up stands only a random chance of success. A year or two from now, after these schools have been shaken and billions of dollars have been poured into unfounded models of improvement, the Obama administration will have to answer for why we've seen so little of the improvement envisioned.

Chapter Fifteen

GETTING THE FEDERAL ROLE BACK ON TRACK

The federal government does, in fairness, have an important role to play in the education of our nation's students. In this context, it bears a major responsibility for upholding the common good of its people, ensuring that the quality of education prepares students to maintain our economic standing in a rapidly changing international environment. The federal government also has a responsibility to promote and embrace free public education as the cornerstone of our freedom and our democratic way of life. Furthermore, it bears a major obligation to ferret out discriminatory practices in our public schools based on race, gender, disability, and sexual orientation. Over the last several decades federal involvement has been significant and successful in these areas. An additional responsibility is embedded in ensuring, to the extent possible, that equal educational opportunities exist for all students. To achieve this goal, the federal government has for many years made significant financial commitments—as evidenced by such initiatives as Title I and the Individuals with Disabilities Education Act.

Yes, the federal government does have a broad and important role in our nation's public schools, but tension has risen dramatically over the past fifteen to twenty years in regard to how it carries out that role while at the same time respecting the roles of state governments, the education community, and local school boards.

The recommendations that follow are intended to convey a vision for a future in which the federal government, states, and local school districts can work in harmony, respecting each other's respective roles and areas of responsibility.

RECOMMENDATION 1: PROVIDE RESEARCH-BASED FEDERAL RECOMMENDATIONS TO INFORM STATE-BASED SCHOOL REFORM

The federal government should regularly provide a series of research-based, policy-driven recommendations to states and districts. Such recommendations should convey a validated reform platform, be aligned with identified good practice, and have the potential to improve student learning. States and districts should then be "turned loose" to determine the extent to which the recommendations should be considered, and to decide how to implement them.

Like a helicopter in the sky, the federal government has a great overall view of the national landscape from which to craft national education policy to support states and districts. Examples of past successes in this area include the desegregation of schools, protecting the rights of students with special needs, and funding programs to address unequal opportunities. Even No Child Left Behind (NCLB) offers examples of important policy directions for public education, including the disaggregation of student data, regular reporting of student progress to parents, calling for educator accountability, and promoting the need to improve teacher preparation. For all of these efforts and accomplishments, the federal government rightfully deserves recognition and appreciation.

The problem develops when the federal government confuses policy direction with nonnegotiable mandates. Let me offer one specific example of a federally driven and Reagan administration–endorsed publication, *A Nation at Risk*, that had a profound impact on public education without ever amounting to a mandate. Research Scientist Carl Sunderman reports: "This was a reform movement where within two years of the publication of *A Nation at Risk*, most states had initiated or enacted some of the educational reforms suggested in the report—without federal fiscal initiatives attached."[1] This report has served to generate numerous state education reforms over the years. I can speak personally to the impact of this report in energizing a discourse on public education within a state. I was appointed as Connecticut's commissioner of education on the very day (April 26, 1983) that *A Nation at Risk* was released.

This report gave me a major opportunity to challenge many of the long-established laws, practices, and programs dominating the state's educational landscape at that time. Furthermore, the report's recommendations served as a wake-up call to the state legislature and the state board of education concerning the need for change. With a focused agenda for change, developed with the full support of all of the various education and community groups, the Connecticut legislature in 1986 passed one of the most comprehensive school reform packages in the country. The Education Enhancement Act (EEA), as the legislation was named, was overwhelmingly supported by a Republican-controlled legislature, working cooperatively with a governor who was a Democrat. This outcome was definitely an example of political cooperation and commitment, unlike the partisan politics practiced in the present U.S. Congress.

The new legislation provided $300 million to fund its school reform initiatives, with the largest percentage of the money dedicated to improving teaching. It focused on raising teacher salaries and improving teacher preparation, induction, and professional development. In addition, the legislation instituted the state's first statewide testing program, raised high school graduation course requirements, and served to elevate Connecticut's standing as a leader in school reform. This one state-specific example points to the great potential that exists for successful education reform when reform initiatives are implemented at the local level, have the support of a state's various constituent groups and political leaders, and energize a statewide resolve to improve the state's system of public education. I would characterize the EEA as a real success story in Connecticut, emanating from a federally driven policy report. The important lesson here is that Connecticut was not told what to do and how to do it by the federal government—but rather was motivated by a federal policy report (*A Nation at Risk*) to consider, in its deliberations, a series of its own policy and

program recommendations, identified in the EEA legislation Contrast the buy-in that occurred in Connecticut
(evidenced by all the various constituent groups' coalescing
behind the legislation)—and with other state-driven reforms
that have occurred over the years—to states' responses to the
onerous mandates of NCLB, Race to the Top (RTT), and
School Improvement Grants (SIG).

RECOMMENDATION 2: REAUTHORIZE AND REFORM NCLB—NOW!

Congress must coalesce and develop a bipartisan commitment to moving forward on the reauthorization and the
reform of NCLB. They need to put aside political considerations in addressing the many components of the legislation,
especially those that are flawed and in need of correction.
Numerous groups and organizations have put forth specific recommendations, the majority of which are similar in
intent, and which should serve as the foundation on which
Congress can build as it moves forward.

I must pause here to remind those responsible for crafting the new legislation to put aside any consideration of
the unrealistic comments of former secretary of education
Margaret Spellings, who in 2009 famously quipped, "I talk
about NCLB like Ivory soap: it's 99% pure." She further
noted that "the law simply needs tweaking."[2] Fast-forward
to 2013: here I must remind congressional leaders that this
law needs a major overhaul and cannot be modified by
a series of "tweaks." There is now an urgent need to "fix" a
misguided federal education law—our nation's students and
educators deserve no less.

RECOMMENDATION 3: PROMOTE CIVIC ENGAGEMENT IN SCHOOL REFORM IMPROVEMENT INITIATIVES

The Obama administration should openly and supportively encourage states to conduct a series of ongoing educational forums involving all of the state's key constituent groups, including teachers, administrators, parents, students, school board members, legislators, and members of the business community. The forums should be designed to engage the participants in an open dialogue surrounding the condition of education in the state, the formulation of policy directions, and the strategies to be used to improve the state's public education system. In addition, the states should be expected to affix specific timelines for the implementation of the strategies and, to the extent possible, assign responsibilities for follow-up actions (to the state department of education, the state legislature, union organizations, school boards, PTAs, chambers of commerce, and so on).

A state's engagement of its constituent groups, encouraged at the federal level, could lead to a coordinated statewide effort to address school improvement. The collaboration of diverse individuals and groups charged with addressing the issues of their public schools would allow a state's constituents to move aggressively forward on a common course of action to improve the state's schools. The power of public sentiment, often translated through public discourse, cannot be ignored in the pursuit of the resolution of long-standing problems. The words of Abraham Lincoln ring true here: "Public sentiment is everything. With public sentiment, nothing can fail, without it nothing can succeed."[3]

The importance of communication cannot be overemphasized—a truth that regrettably has not been put into practice by the Obama administration, the U.S. Department of Education (ED), and Congress. Rather, they have chosen a course of developing school reform initiatives in a vacuum—void of any input from teachers, administrators, parents, and school board members. Federal engagement in school reform would have traveled a very different path, and gained greater public support, had the "federal players" been more open in their approach and responsive to public engagement and discourse. Lester Thurow, former dean at the Massachusetts Institute of Technology, highlights the power of communication in comments concerning global economic change—remarks that have meaning for school reformers: "We are going to have to change our culture to retain our status as the world's preeminent power. We have to talk with one another if we are going to change old attitudes. We must listen to one another in order to change the system."[4]

Jamie Vollmer, in his recent book *Schools Cannot Do It Alone*, places additional emphasis on the necessity and urgency of fostering public engagement in transforming our nation's public schools, calling for "The Great Conversation." He envisions such a conversation "as an ongoing discussion between educators and the communities they serve." He continues, "It is my strongest recommendation that The Great Conversation becomes an integral part of any effort to restructure our schools . . . We must do this in every community, and we must do it now."[5]

My focus with this recommendation is on encouraging the Obama administration and Congress to promote, in the states, the necessary and long-overdue local conversations needed to enhance the quality of education in our nation's public schools. I further encourage the Obama administration and Congress to display the commitment to supporting those education intervention strategies that are developed and implemented within the states. In effect, they must respect the intention of our founders—embedded in our Constitution—and acknowledge that public education is a state responsibility.

RECOMMENDATION 4: HOLD STATES AND SCHOOL DISTRICTS ACCOUNTABLE FOR STUDENT ACHIEVEMENT

The Obama administration should hold governors, chief state school officers, and state boards of education responsible for the condition of public education in their state. Such responsibility has been conferred on these state government officials by their respective state constitutions. Rather than extending its "federal arm" into local schools, the Obama administration would do better to hold states accountable for the quality of education therein—a practice with greater potential for taking broad-based school reform to scale.

The Obama administration needs to assess carefully its role in school reform, stepping back and accepting the reality that the secretary of education cannot attempt to function as the nation's superintendent of schools, and that neither the ED nor Congress can act as the nation's school board. The realities are as follows: our Constitution does not support such a high degree of federal authority over schools as there is now, the funding burden to support public education is disproportionally carried by state and local governments, and states and local school boards bear the major responsibility for the education of our nation's students.

Also, the Obama administration should no longer allow policy gurus, corporate executives, and philanthropic foundation staff to assume so much control in shaping national education policy—including the NCLB, RTT, and SIG initiatives. These individuals essentially have no "on-the-ground" working knowledge of the day-to-day operation of public schools, and they are not conversant with the myriad complexities of classroom teaching and student learning. It is truly unconscionable for the Obama administration to allow these external groups and organizations to have such an influence over our nation's public schools.

In addition, it defies logic for the ED to extend its reach such that it holds individual schools accountable for student progress, completely bypassing the responsibility and authority of state departments of education and state boards of education, and completely ignoring the responsibility for local control entrusted to local school boards. The absurdity of such an elongated federal reach into the operation of local schools is compounded when it is considered that the ED does not have the staff, resources, or expertise to monitor the mandates it has imposed. Ironically, the ED expects the states and school districts—the very entities it has ignored in promoting its agenda—to be accountable for managing the onerous burdens that misguided federal reform strategies have placed on schools.

States, in assuming additional accountability for student achievement, should place a high premium on continued academic advancement on the National Assessment of Educational Progress, which is considered the nation's report card for student achievement, and which is the only tool available for gathering consistent and comparable assessment data. In the future, the National Common Core Standards, when the linked assessments are fully implemented in the states, can also provide comparative student achievement data for state accountability purposes. Additional accountability measures for monitoring student achievement should, at the very least, include state data pertaining to

- School completion rates
- Student attendance
- College acceptance
- The percentage of students participating in Advanced Placement and International Baccalaureate courses
- SAT and ACT scores
- Suspension rates and expulsion rates
- Incidences of school violence
- Indicators of teacher and principal quality (including turnover rates)
- Teacher salary ranges

Furthermore, the states should be required to present all data in a disaggregated format, ensuring that all information is reported by gender, race, ethnicity, and poverty indicators (including the percentage of students receiving free or reduced-price lunch). States should then be required to issue an annual "state report card" for each school district, using all of the achievement data points just listed. A logical next step in this type of accountability model would be for the federal government to issue a biannual "national report card" incorporating the same achievement data points used in the states.

A system of regular state and national reporting on student achievement—using consistent and comparable data—will generate significant public, congressional, and legislative interest. The expectation would be that this consistent and validated assessment information would have its greatest impact as a diagnostic tool to be used by states and school districts to improve student academic progress. What is more, such data reporting would ideally drive additional fiscal resources to those school districts and schools with the greatest identified academic needs.

Holding states accountable for student performance—and having access to timely and comparative state and national achievement data—would allow members of Congress to more accurately assess the condition of education in their respective states. This information would also alert them to the necessity of working more closely with their respective state government officials and their constituents in crafting a school improvement agenda.

This means that the Obama administration, in assessing the status of public education in the nation, needs to move away from a myopic focus on individual school-based improvement. Rather, it should direct its energy and resources toward holding states accountable for statewide improvement in student achievement. Consider that the Obama administration has many fiscal resources at its disposal, which it can use to reward states for consistent improvement in student outcomes and for closing the achievement gap. In turn, if the political will exists in

Congress, the Obama administration could withhold some level of funding to those states that are continually failing to meet their responsibilities in regard to improving student achievement. This becomes a difficult threshold to cross in that some states, those with the greatest financial needs, could lose funding. However, if states are to be held accountable for demonstrated student progress, the federal government will need some means of placing added "pressure" on these states. The Obama administration must have serious discussions with governors and legislative representatives from these states to develop a workable plan that will address the financial implications—while also ensuring the improvement of student achievement.

The challenge is for the federal government to abandon its accountability presence in school reform and to place the burden where it belongs—on state governments. Peter Drucker succinctly captures the essence of this new accountability challenge and imperative recommended for the Obama administration: "What you have to do and the way you choose do it is incredibly simple. Whether or not you choose to do it, that's another matter."[6]

RECOMMENDATION 5: PROVIDE LEADERSHIP IN EDUCATION RESEARCH

The ED is well positioned to play a major role in research aimed at identifying educational practices and programs that have proven effective. This is an appropriate and significant role for the ED, and would address a long-standing need on the part of our nation's teachers and administrators. It is a national embarrassment that there is such a dearth of substantive education research—and that filling this research gap does appear to be a high priority. The federal government has the capacity to be a national repository for and disseminator of education research through its Institute of Education Sciences and the recently established What Works Clearinghouse, through a reordering of its funding priorities, and by soliciting grant proposals from a broad network of university research providers. State governments and local school districts do not have the staff, funds, or expertise to initiate major research initiatives. In effect, they are not in a position to fill the research void. Instead, they place this long-overdue need for timely and substantive research on the doorstep of the ED.

Some of the major research areas that should be a high priority include the following:

Reading

Research in this area entails documentation of approaches to the teaching of reading, including the identification of best practices at the elementary, middle school, and high school levels. Further research is clearly needed in the area of adolescent reading in particular, given that eight million adolescents do not read at grade level. Despite this glaring deficiency in a critical basic skill area, there is a minimal body of research to inform teacher pedagogy and curricula and highlight professional development needs at the middle and high school levels.

Mathematics and Science

Such research includes identifying successful strategies in the teaching of mathematics and science, with an emphasis on the elementary grades. There is a long history of poor teaching and inadequate curricula in these subject areas in grades 1 through 6, a period of time when the essential foundations for mathematics and science are established—foundations that are the precursors to success in these subjects in the high school years.

Brain Research

Education researchers should make better use of what the emerging body of brain research is telling us about how the human brain works and the implications for teaching and learning. An immediate question needs to be asked: To understand how the brain works, would you go to a teacher? Probably not! As one teacher reportedly noted, "I can count on one hand the times I directly studied about the brain in college . . . I probably can count the number of times on one finger!" But as John Medina notes in *Brain Rules*, "Brain research is to teaching and learning as anatomy is to the practice of medicine."[7] The irony is that we seek services every day from such specialists as doctors, lawyers, electricians, architects . . . and the list goes on. And yet, the very "specialists" (teachers) to whom parents entrust their children daily have little if any understanding of how the human brain works and its direct impact on how children learn. Nor are they conversant on the subject of how brain research–based teaching strategies can enhance student achievement.

The ED should be a major repository for the most up-to-date research on the human brain, clearly identifying the teaching methodologies and learning modalities that are derived from such research. The research findings should be disseminated on a regular basis to teachers, administrations, and teacher preparation programs. I would argue that brain research should be the driving force, the catalyst, for all of the ED's school reform efforts. The ED could offer leadership in brain research as a new route to follow in pursuit of a substantive reform agenda.

Best Practices in Teaching

Research should include the identification of best practices in teaching, signifying a move away from a commitment to highly qualified teachers and toward a commitment to highly effective teachers. The ED should be at the forefront of developing a comprehensive and research-based agenda to identify the skill sets and the delivery methodology—the artistry of teaching—needed to enhance teacher efficacy and student learning. Such research should be grounded in case studies of highly effective teachers and their practices.

The ED should make available, on a much larger scale than is presently the case, videos of effective teaching practice, and should gather a collection of "stories" of effective practitioners. The ED should also make grant awards to states to enable outstanding teachers to conduct workshops—

a direction that will, over time, produce some of the best available research. The key point is that solid information on quality teaching is not gleaned from textbooks or university lectures, but rather from examining teachers at work, understanding what they do and how they do it.

The ED already has access to an enormous research base on which it regrettably has failed to capitalize—the National Board for Professional Teaching Standards. This body of over one hundred thousand National Board Certified Teachers, each of whom has gone through a lengthy, comprehensive, and validated assessment, represents a major untapped resource for identifying exemplars of the teaching profession. It is difficult to comprehend why the ED has not expended the time and resources to identify the qualities, skills, and attributes underlying the successes of educators within this mother lode of teaching excellence.

Research supports the value inherent in gaining an improved ability to "know great teaching when you see it," understanding the conditions that underlie such exemplary practice, and providing the fiscal resources to allow states and districts to implement cited best practices to exponentially scale up effective teaching. The ED should engage researchers who understand that their research projects should focus on what happens in the classroom, and not on esoteric ideologies. I heard a story several years ago that succinctly makes this point: "A researcher visited a classroom characterized by outstanding student achievement and great teaching. While impressed with the outcomes he had witnessed, the researcher questioned whether or not what he had witnessed in practice would work in theory!"

Enough said about those who continue to offer a research perspective that is far removed from where teaching and learning take place—in the classroom.

Identification of High-Performing Schools

Research should focus on schools that have moved from being low performing to exhibiting high performance, generating evaluative and research data outlining the specific strategies and programs used to transform the schools. There are several well-known examples of "turnaround schools" from which the ED—although cognizant of their existence—has gleaned little information in regard to the personnel, program, and curriculum changes that underlie these schools' success stories. It is also important to note that the ED conducts various awards programs to celebrate school-based excellence on an annual basis. Yet organizing such celebratory events, although they serve a noble purpose, is far less important than identifying the factors leading to the success of these schools. The reality is that nationally recognized turnaround schools and various other identified models of "schools of excellence" do not have the resources, time, or energy to focus on conducting research into their own high levels of achievement. The reality is that they are too busy devoting their attention—and rightly so—to their ongoing school improvement endeavors. These success stories provide the ED with a significant opportunity to use its resources and funds to launch research initiatives to delineate what sets these schools apart as beacons of excellence—and later to disseminate the findings to states, districts, and schools across the country.

The identification of a number of examples of school improvement programs that have been highly successful makes a strong case for conducting ongoing research into the practices therein. The potential knowledge base that further research could help create would serve to inform significantly the ongoing discourse on school reform. The National Association of Secondary School Principals (NASSP) has over the past seven years identified sixty Breakthrough Schools (BTSs) as part of a national project to identify middle and high schools that have overcome a long-standing record of low academic performance. These same schools, over time, have shown marked improvement in student achievement. Although NASSP has been able to provide some basic information about the key factors leading to the success of the BTSs, the association has not been able to generate the necessary outside funding to mount a comprehensive research initiative.

This is a frustrating outcome when a "treasure trove" of research opportunities exists, especially concerning turnaround secondary schools—for which there is a dearth of research. On several occasions the BTSs were brought to the attention of ED staff with an expectation, never realized, that these staff would be interested in providing assistance and support to gain a greater understanding of how these schools "broke ranks" with other low-performing middle and high schools. Such a research-based initiative would serve to inform secondary school practice and programs in the pursuit of school improvement.

In summary, the ED should commit major funding to education research, and should make this commitment a cornerstone of its efforts to improve schools. The department should devote its energy to promoting research that

- Informs excellence in teaching
- Provides models of successful schools, informing critical areas of instruction (reading, mathematics, and science in particular)
- Provides updated information on evolving brain science and the implications for teaching and learning

Following such long-overdue directions would elevate the status of the ED and provide a pathway that educators would be willing to travel as full partners.

RECOMMENDATION 6: PROMOTE PRESCHOOL AND EARLY CHILDHOOD EDUCATION

The federal government should provide major financial support to foster the growth of preschool and early childhood education initiatives. The majority of school reformers attend solely to grades K through 12, completely missing the importance and imperativeness of preschool education. The ED has only recently come to the table in stressing preschool as a major component of its reform agenda. Although its 2011 RTT early childhood education competitive grant program is laudable, it falls far short of the high-level commitment needed to ensure that all preschoolers have access to high-quality programs. Such a heightened commitment would serve to nurture their development and more adequately prepare them for entry into school.

Consider the reality that the new RTT initiative is competitive, meaning that only a small number of states and children will benefit. It is important to point out that a genuine national commitment to early childhood education would entail major new (noncompetitive) funding going directly to states and districts. A financial commitment of the type envisioned here would allow parents and early childhood providers, within the states, to develop and implement programs and services to better address the needs of our youngest children.

Another giant step for the Obama administration would be to fully fund Head Start, a federally funded program first implemented in the Johnson administration in the 1960s and intended to provide our neediest preschoolers with access to age-appropriate programs, activities, and health services. These offerings, in turn, would provide them with a "head start" in life. Regrettably, to date only about 45 percent of eligible children are reaping the benefits of this program, access to which was initially promised to all eligible children. This represents the type of long-term investment that legislators and federal officials have failed to support over the years. Such leaders live in a world of "instant gratification," needing their policies to have an immediate impact rather than grasping the reality that investments in such programs as Head Start can have significant, lasting gains. These lasting benefits would promote greater educational opportunity for our nation's most vulnerable children.

There are numerous studies and nationally representative data that show disparities in cognition, social-emotional development, and health status between financially disadvantaged, at-risk children and more advantaged children at as early as nine months of age. Other research data lead to the conclusion that these disparities become greater as children grow older. Still other studies provide the Obama administration and Congress with additional evidence of the long-term economic benefits of Head Start and other early childhood programs. Now consider the continuing longitudinal University of North Carolina study, started in 1972, that found that at-risk children who participated in an early childhood program were two and a half times more likely to be attending a four-year college or university at age twenty-one than those who did not participate.[8]

If federal policymakers and legislators require more evidence, they need to review data from the widely acclaimed High/Scope Educational Research Foundation study, which found that at-risk children in a Michigan preschool program were 44 percent more likely to graduate from high school than those who did not attend such a program.[9] This finding alone should "awaken" the educational critics who continually lament the high dropout rates in our schools, sending a clear message that addressing the dropout issue at the secondary school level may very well be an exercise in futility, given that the problem's true genesis may reside in the preschool years. This conclusion is supported by a major and eye-opening study of preschool children that substantiates, through scientific research, the direct link between children's early learning and their later intellectual growth, regardless of their race.[10] After extensive observations in the homes of children from both low-income and affluent families, the researchers concluded that children from lower socioeconomic backgrounds had a vocabulary of two to three thousand fewer words, on average, than those of children from affluent backgrounds. This finding exposes the significant disadvantage confronting children from lower socioeconomic backgrounds on their entry into kindergarten—a disadvantage exacerbated by the reality that school districts "wait" until a minimum age of five to allow entry into kindergarten. The children with the greatest needs, who have grown up in low-income households and are at a significant vocabulary disadvantage, essentially wait on the sidelines to enter kindergarten, causing them to potentially fall even further behind other children in their school readiness. It borders on hypocrisy for states and school districts to have such outdated school entry policies at a time when they should be developing highly individualized policies to allow the students with the greatest needs to enter school at an earlier age.

This problem is further compounded by the reality that the majority of kindergarten classes are half-day programs (two and a half hours on average), and that class sizes generally vary from twenty to twenty-five students per class. Consider the plight of—and unrealistic expectations for—kindergarten teachers who conduct both a morning and an afternoon session with a total daily enrollment of forty to fifty students, and who are asked to individualize instruction! This has even more serious implications for those teachers who teach in lower-socioeconomic communities, a large number of whose students enter school with significant vocabulary deficits. Meeting the needs of these students is an onerous task for even the most accomplished teachers.

As the Obama administration and Congress contemplate their future commitment to addressing the preschool issues identified here, they also need to consider the equity and inequality resulting from the long-standing underfunding of Head Start. These concerns are made worse by the reality that affluent parents have the resources to enroll their children in high-quality preschool programs at a very early age, and for extended periods of time. These parents are ensuring that their children will have a "running start" in their preparation for school entry. This condition serves to further widen the achievement gap for students from low-income families, whose parents must wait for federal support to allow their children to compete on a level playing field. Unless the disparities and unfairness in early childhood opportunities are addressed, closing the achievement gap and decreasing the dropout rate will remain distant goals—and, as a nation, we will face a continuing divide in our schools between the "haves" and "have-nots."

Hubert Humphrey eloquently captured the imperative of making a national commitment to those in our society with the greatest needs: "The moral test of Government is how the Government treats those in the dawn of life, the children; those who are in the twilight of life, the elderly; and those who are in the shadows of life, the sick, the needy and the handicapped."[11] Humphrey offered a major challenge to our national leaders to address the needs of our nation's children and other groups in our society. Of particular note is his emphasis on the government's responsibility to accept this challenge. Unless this responsibility is acted on, those in the "dawn of life," our nation's children, especially those with the greatest needs, will face a difficult future—an outcome that will lie at the feet of those who failed the "moral test."

The federal government should fully fund Head Start, making sure that all eligible children are enrolled. This funding commitment should be phased in over a five-year period.

This would allow the necessary time to adjust federal funding priorities to do the following:

- Accommodate the necessary and substantial funding increase
- Allow adequate time to train the new staff needed
- Give states and districts time to accommodate the physical space required for a major influx of Head Start students

The Obama administration should use the "bully pulpit" to encourage state and school district leaders to formulate a new mind-set of considering preschool education as a critical component of their respective education systems. To this point, important lessons can be learned from the School of the 21st Century (21C) model, developed at Yale University by Edmund Zigler, often referred to as the "father" of Head Start, and his colleague Matia Finn-Stevenson. In this model, participating public schools are open to preschoolers from 7:00 a.m. until 6:00 p.m. The schools provide the facilities and maintenance support for the program, and community organizations provide the staffing and program oversight. Parents and community organizations supply the necessary funding, using a need-based tuition formula for entry into the program. This model has been expanding across the country, and Springfield, Missouri, is widely recognized as a national example for its long-standing involvement in and commitment to 21C schools.

There are other examples of enlightened school leadership that have resulted in expanded school-based preschool opportunities—which in turn have offered working models to promote greater coherence for children between the pre-school and primary grade years. More state and local leaders need a "push," a greater awakening to the imperative of providing services for very young children. To increase the potential for this push and awakening to occur, the Obama administration should send a loud and clear message of its unwavering support for increased funding and enhanced community involvement and commitment. A message of this type has the potential to foster greater support from state and local leaders to promote preschool education. Such a message ought to recognize and commend the staff, parents, and community members who have already demonstrated their ongoing commitment to our nation's youngest children.

RECOMMENDATION 7: PROMOTE COMMUNITY EDUCATION

The ED should stimulate, through a variety of competitive grant programs, a dramatic expansion of community education programs in our nation's schools. Although there has been a federal commitment to funding the 21st Century Community Learning Centers grant for the last decade, the grant has been level funded (no increase or decrease)—at approximately $1 million—since 2009. The ED allocates this relatively small budget for supporting extended school day and evening programs for students, parents, and community members at the same time that it remains aggressive in infusing billions of dollars of funding into its signature RTT and SIG initiatives. There needs to be a greater aware-ness in the ED of the significance of community education programs and the related impact that such programs have on the "total life" of a school.

I had the opportunity to serve as the principal of Conte Community School (K–8) in New Haven, Connecticut, in the late 1960s. This school had a low-income population that made up approximately 50 percent of the student body. The school was open from 8:00 a.m to 10:00 p.m. every day, and also had extended weekend hours. This was definitely not a traditional school in that it provided a plethora of after-school services, including tutoring classes, adult education courses, arts and physical education programs, neighborhood forums, a health clinic, and a variety of social services for the community. Many of these programs and services were also offered during the regular school day.

In addition, during the school week both dental and medical checkups were available to students. Having two full-time nurses from the Visiting Nurse Association further supported these health services, with both nurses taking turns spending 50 percent of their time in the school and 50 percent of their time in the community. One nurse was always on duty in the school, while the other nurse worked in the homes of the school's population. This unique arrangement allowed for the provision of comprehensive and continuous health services to the students and their families. The school also had two school community workers—both of whom were indigenous to the school's community—who facilitated a direct and continuing relationship and partnership between the school and its parents and community. They also bore the responsibility for operating a nonprofit secondhand clothing store on the school's campus, providing free clothing, that was widely used by members of the community.

The school campus also housed a library, staffed by the city's public library system, serving both the general public and the school. Further, the campus had a separate facility for senior citizens, which allowed for intergenerational interaction between the seniors and the students. In fact, many of the seniors acted as tutors and "advisers" to the student body—functions that they carried out in an exemplary manner.

It is important to point out that a majority of the extended-day programs were fully funded by other City of New Haven departments, including the parks and recreation department, senior services, the health department, the public library system, and various other city-funded social agencies. The school system itself provided the physical plant and bore the responsibility for maintenance of that location. The city, in turn, provided staff and resources to service the multitude of programs and activities of which students, parents, and community members could avail themselves. An important by-product of this school district–city partnership was that municipal funds did not have to be expended for the renovation and building of new facilities to accommodate programs and services that could be housed in public school buildings. This reduced the duplication of services and the need for new facilities, resulting in savings for taxpayers. Conte Community School in particular received both national and international recognition for the scope and breadth of its programming, but it is important to point out that the City of New Haven and the school district had a citywide commitment to community schools, and that over time a significant number of other schools were converted to function as community education centers.

The success of Conte Community School cannot be overstated. Its students performed very well academically, school suspensions and other disciplinary measures were at a minimum, and parent support was overwhelming high. In addition, teacher turnover was almost nonexistent, community participation was robust, and the school served as a widely recognized model for school reform.

One of the truly great examples of the school's success and the unwavering support it received from its community occurred during the late 1960s, when New Haven was host to the famous Black Panther trials. During this difficult time the city was in wretched turmoil: military personnel and police patrolled the streets, major rioting occurred, and significant damage was inflicted on a number of stores and public buildings. During this same period, Conte Community School did not sustain damage of any kind. This reality takes on added significance when it is considered that bands of hostile marauders moved past the school on a regular basis during this tumultuous period. Not one school window was broken, graffiti did not appear on the school's walls, and violence never erupted on the school campus. I believed then, and I believe now, that the school was immune to damage and violence because it was recognized as a true community haven and a beacon of hope for the community's future—and that it belonged to the community!

Although Conte Community School flourished for several years, it largely met the fate of many models of innovation and success. As state and local budgets were cut and state and federal mandates forced districts to focus on basic skills attainment, innovative programs, such as community school initiatives, were eliminated or reduced in scope. It is my understanding, as of this writing, that Conte Community School still attempts to function as a community-centered school, yet the present iteration probably pales in comparison to what it was in the school's heyday. During its peak time it arguably represented the finest example of a school and its community coming together for common purposes, working toward both the improvement of the quality of education in the school and the betterment of community life.

Why do I spend extensive time extolling the virtues of community schools? I should point out that I also experienced community education as a Mott Fellow in this field, working in Flint, Michigan, the birthplace of community schools, and simultaneously earning my PhD at Michigan State University with a focus in this area. I have also been a disciple of James Comer, a nationally and internationally known professor of child psychology at Yale University, renowned for his seminal work on the Comer School Development Program. This model, used in schools throughout the nation, focuses on the inextricable link between schools and the parents and communities they serve. Comer's main thesis is that schools and communities are really one larger entity, and that school success is directly linked to engaging with parents and members of the community. An old African proverb brings into clear focus what has been affectionately termed the "Comer Model": "It takes a whole village to raise a child." In many ways the community schools concept and the Comer Model are in agreement on the need for a vision of public education that expands beyond school walls.

My emphasis on community schools is also intended to send a clear message to the Obama administration, the ED, and Congress concerning the urgent need to refocus fiscal priorities—and to foster a greater understanding that public schools alone cannot address the complex and myriad societal problems and issues that many students, especially needy students, bring with them to school. They need to grasp that the schoolhouse represents a citadel of hope and the potential to galvanize the support and commitment of parents and the larger community in the pursuit of equal educational opportunity for all students. It ultimately is the "village" of the school that creates a climate of trust within which students and community members can flourish. This is the promise, this is the vision, that community education brings to the table of school reform, and around which the decision makers in Washington DC need to rally their support.

The Obama administration should provide significant fiscal resources for competitive grants to states and districts to enhance existing community school programs and allow for the development of new initiatives in this area. This grant funding should also be available to those districts and schools that have demonstrated a long-standing commitment to community schools, and in which "models of excellence" exist. Grants of this type would give these districts and schools the requisite resources to serve as "living laboratories," affording educators, school boards, parents, and community groups access to working models of successful community school programs. Through such a process, there would be a greater potential to scale up this initiative to districts and schools across the nation.

I once again ask the Obama administration to use its bully pulpit, this time to energize the national discourse surrounding the imperative for schools, parents, and community members to come together to promote both student excellence and community enhancement. They must support using the school building as the launching pad—as the locus for such action. What is more, the Obama administration must put forth a clarion call to governors, chief state school officers, school superintendents, and school board members, alerting them to the need for enlightened leadership to promote public use of school facilities. The message should include the importance of opening the school doors wide to allow for greater community support for public education, and of publicizing to community members the benefits realized from local tax dollars.

There needs to be a continuing national reminder that public schools, by their very nature, are public, and are not the sole province of local school boards and superintendents. In fact, whenever a school closes its doors at 3:00 or 3:30 every afternoon and on weekends, it is wasting taxpayer dollars. This reality deprives the community of valuable space for its own programs and activities, and makes the school seem more isolated and removed from the community. It also divests the school of the opportunity to generate community-based resources and support for the school and its students. If ever there was a time for a vocal and sustained "voice" advocating for community schools, it is now.

RECOMMENDATION 8: PROMOTE EXPANDED SUMMER SCHOOL PROGRAMS

The Obama administration should make available substantial grant monies to reward those school districts that have made a commitment to offering expanded summer learning opportunities for students, and even larger competitive grants to stimulate a major expansion of academic summer school initiatives. Taking into consideration the enormous amount of funding required for such a new commitment, I would recommend that the focus of such funding be placed on two priority areas:

1. Children in grades K through 4, who are attaining basic skills, with emphasis given to directing funding to the poorest communities, in which summer school education is almost nonexistent
2. Those students in middle and high school who have fallen far below normal grade-level expectations, and who may be tomorrow's school dropouts if they do not receive intensive academic intervention opportunities (summer school)

In other words, I recommend that funding be targeted toward enhancing opportunities for students in the formative years of learning, our students with the greatest academic needs, and students who are on the precipice of school failure.

There exists an extensive body of research that supports providing summer school programs for students. This research speaks clearly to the importance of summer school education for students in need of remedial assistance, especially in the areas of reading, language arts, and mathematics —and to the significant impact such programs can have on reducing "summer loss" (falling further behind in academic achievement), especially for low-income students. Consider the recent Rand Corporation study, funded by the Wallace Foundation, that "confirms that students who attend summer programs can disrupt the learning loss and do better in school than their peers who do not attend the same programs."[12] Nancy Devine, director of communication at the Wallace Foundation, offers the following insightful observation in responding to the study: "About 80% of a child's waking hours are spent outside of school, and summer is a large chunk of that time." She added, based on the Wallace Foundation's further review of the study, that "it is increasingly clear to us that the six-hour-long school day, 180 day school year is not enough to give disadvantaged children the education that they deserve."[13]

It truly is amazing that the practice of a significant number of public schools of shutting down their facilities during the summer months has endured. Public schools operate in a context imbued with the egregious and illogical assumption that learning only takes place within a nine-and-a-half-month school year. Such an assumption completely disregards the reality that students who are not caught up on their academic studies will fall even further behind as a result of this practice. This summer loss has its most profound impact on students from lower socioeconomic backgrounds and students who are English language learners.

A quote from Medina's *Brain Rules* can be used to expand on the significant disruption in the learning process resulting from schools' "taking the summer off." Medina borrows a comment from the foundational work of Hermann Ebbinghaus, which makes the point that "people usually forget about 90% of what they learn in a class within 30 days." Medina adds that "this forgetting occurs within the first few hours after class," reporting that these findings have been "robustly" confirmed over time.[14] Consider the impact on students, who are so likely to forget what they have learned in only a short period of time, when they are given approximately seventy-five days off annually in between learning experiences!

The reality of summer loss also has huge implications for the goal of closing the achievement gap between economically advantaged and disadvantaged students. Students from more affluent families are exposed to a number of summer learning and enhancement activities and programs, including academic tutoring; exposure to the arts; family travel excursions; engagement in structured physical activities; and, in many cases, exposure to country club atmospheres and the related enhancement activities offered. Students from less affluent families generally stay within the confines of their neighborhood and have little if any opportunity to engage in learning or enhancement activities. The old adage "The rich get richer and the poor get poorer" applies to our nation's students, for whom the achievement gap continues to widen as those students exposed to summer learning opportunities advance and those who do not fall even further behind.

It is truly perplexing that the national discourse on closing the achievement gap confines its focus to a traditional 180-day school year. To expand on this point, consider that the major funding expenditures for Title I, RTT, and the SIG initiative have been directed to traditional school day and year programs and initiatives. It appears that very little attention is given to the direct causative and cumulative effect on our nation's schools and students of the extensive summer respite granted every year. This annual break translates into a collective loss of approximately thirty months of schooling over the course of a K–12 school experience. Taken a step further, this represents approximately 900 days of lost opportunities for student learning. As a nation committed to equal educational opportunities for all students, we can no longer tolerate the "learning avoidance" inherent in our outdated 180-day school year.

I also recommend that the Obama administration send forth a strong message to state and local school district leaders concerning the importance of public schools' maximizing their use of the summer months—another viable tool to be added to their set of student improvement strategies.

I predict that this recommendation will be well received in states and school districts, but I also acknowledge that opening schools for summer learning is not a fiscally viable option for most states and local school districts at this time. Faced with this reality, the federal government would do well to offer financial assistance in this area, as states and school districts would accept this as an appropriate role for the federal government to play in school reform.

A FINAL WORD

To those who argue that, given our nation's current fiscal crisis, there isn't sufficient funding for these recommendations: I remind you that the Obama administration has allocated billions of dollars to fund programs like RTT and SIG. As discussed previously, this huge commitment of federal dollars has gone to fund initiatives that have no viable research base, create problems in schools and school districts, and represent an unwelcome usurping of local control of public education. In addition, the competitive nature of these grants has meant that they have benefitted only a small number of states, schools, and students; the nonfunded states have essentially been relegated to the sidelines of federal school reform efforts. One can only imagine what the impact of these billions of dollars would have been if the funding streams had been directed to education research, preschool and early childhood education, and "throwing open" the doors of our nation's schools to allow them to function as community education centers. Moreover, this funding could have provided much-needed resources for promoting civic engagement in school reform at the state and local levels, implementing and expanding student summer school opportunities, and launching a significant commitment to developing school reform policies that have a greater potential to enhance student learning.

CONCLUSION

There are going to be times when we can't wait
for somebody. Now you're either on the bus or
off the bus.

Ken Kesey[1]

This is a critical time in American public education.
School reform initiatives abound, emerging from many
directions and from a diverse group of reform initiators. The
main purpose of this book has been to bring into clear focus
the misguided and ill-informed school reform policies and
strategies affecting our public schools and educators, and to
provide an alternative vision for reforming our education
system, and for consistent and sustainable school improvement. We urgently need to reroute the course of school
reform and to ensure that the "right drivers and passengers"
are on board.

Are there other areas of school reform that could have
been included in the book? The answer is yes. However, I
made a conscious decision to address those areas of school
reform that—to my way of thinking—are primary when
compared to others. Consider my rationale:

- *Teaching.* The book places the highest priority on having
  a quality teacher in every classroom. It is my strong

belief that the teacher is the center of the education universe, and that all school reform initiatives are doomed unless teacher effectiveness and efficacy are at the core of school improvement practices. What is needed is greater engagement of teachers in shaping their profession, and improved practices that can advance teaching and learning.

- *Charter schools.* Although charter schools have become the "hot ticket" for school reform advocates, there is a discrepancy between the scope and purpose of today's charter schools and the initial purpose for which these schools were intended. Charter schools regrettably have evolved into competitors to traditional public schools, draining resources and support. I have offered recommendations that can enhance the future direction of the charter movement, and that are intended to address the need for the charter school advocates to move away from quantity over quality.

- *International student comparisons.* I challenge the notion that the international ranking of a country's students is a fair assessment of student achievement, and maintain that it cannot be used as a predictor of economic growth. Further, I would argue that international student comparisons send a false message concerning student progress, and provide fodder for advancing misguided school improvement practices. My recommendations present a case for moving the focus of such assessments in a new, more positive direction.

- *The federal government's role in school reform.* The federal government, by putting aside the time-honored American tradition of local control, has caused anguish and turmoil among educators, parents, and state and local leaders. I have presented a new vision for the federal role that has the potential to be well received, and that would represent a safe harbor for their future engagement.

It is time for educators to take back their profession—and not allow individuals far removed from schools and classrooms to dictate the terms and conditions of school reform. It is also time to make a decision: either get on the bus that is moving in the direction of a new vision for school improvement, or get off!

ENDNOTES

INTRODUCTION

1. Jim Collins, *Good to Great* (New York: HarperCollins, 2001), 41.

CHAPTER ONE

1. John Gesmonde, "States Mesmerized by Fed's Money: 'Moonwalking' in Advancing Backward School Reform," *Connecticut Association of School Administrators (CASA) Newsletter*, May 2010.
2. Angela Beeley, "Mad as Hell," *Education Week*, April 27, 2011, 33.
3. Ibid.

CHAPTER TWO

1. Spherical Cow, "Linda Darling-Hammond on TFA and Teacher Preparation," *Real Learning Matters* (blog), March 16, 2011, http://reallearningmatters .wordpress.com/2011/03/16/linda-darling -hammond-on-tfa-and-teacher-preparation/.

2. Michael Winerip, "A Chosen Few Are Teaching for America," *New York Times*, July 13, 2010.

3. Darling-Hammond, quoted in Spherical Cow, "Linda Darling-Hammond."

4. Mark Naison, "Teach for America and Me: A Failed Courtship." *With a Brooklyn Accent* (blog), June 22, 2011, http://withabrooklynaccent.blogspot. com/2011/06/teach-for-america-and-me-failed.html.

5. Barbara Miner, "Looking Past the Spin: Teach for America," *Rethinking Schools*, 24, no. 3 (March 24, 2010): 3.

6. Ibid., 10.

7. Ibid.

8. Wendy Puriefoy, quoted in Miner, "Looking Past," 6.

9. Wendy Puriefoy, quoted in Miner, "Looking Past," 6.

10. George H. Wood, "Somebody Explain This to Me," *Forum for Education and Democracy* (blog), June 16, 2010, www.forumforeducation.org/blog/ somebody-explain-me-0.

11. Miner, "Looking Past," 13.

12. Arthur Levine, quoted in Michael Bimbaum, "With Limited Training, TFA Recruits Play an Expanding Role in Schools," *Washington Post*, August 23, 2010.

13. Miner, "Looking Past," 16.

14. Barnett Berry, quoted in Miner, "Looking Past,"5.

15. ECS. "State Notes on Administrator License Requirements, Portability Waivers and Alternate Certification." Education Commission of the States: Denver, Colorado, 2011. (www.ecs.org)

16. Source: UAC R277-505-4, http://www.rules.utah
    .gov/publicat/code/r277/r277-505.htm#T4

17. Source: DOE, Bureau of Credentialing, http://www
    .education.nh.gov/

18. Source: 603 CMR 7.14, http://www.doe.mass.edu/
    lawsregs/603cmr7.html?section=14

19. Source: Florida Statutes 1001.42, http://www.flsenate
    .gov/Laws/Statutes/?from500=yes&CFID=1327906&
    CFTOKEN=79269589#TitleXLVIII

20. Diane Ravitch, *The Death and Life of the Great
    American School System* (New York: Basic Books,
    2010), 192.

CHAPTER THREE

1. W. Edwards Deming, quoted in Gerald N. Tirozzi,
   "Pay for Performance Myths," *NewsLeader* 57, no. 7
   (March 2010): 2.

2. Eva Baker et al., "Problems with the Use of Student
   Test Scores to Evaluate Teachers" (briefing paper,
   Economic Policy Institute, Washington DC, August
   29, 2010), 6.

3. Ibid. Eva Baker, et al., 6

4. Patrick Schuemann and James Guthrie quoted in:
   Tom Toch, "Myths About Paying Good Teachers,"
   Washington Post, October 16, 2009.

5. Sharon Otterman, "NYC abandons Teacher Bonus
   Program," *New York Times*, July 18, 2011.

6. Melanie Moran, "Teacher Performance Pay Alone Does Not Raise Test Scores," National Center on Performance Incentives, Vanderbilt University, Nashville, TN, September 21, 2010, http://news .vanderbilt.edu/2010/09/teacher-performance-pay/.

7. Valerie Straus, "Chicago's Teacher Performance-Based Pay Didn't Work," *Washington Post*, June 1, 2010.

8. William Mathis and Kevin G. Welner, "Assessing the Research Base for a Blueprint for Reform" (policy brief, National Education Policy Center, University of Colorado at Boulder, October 2010).

9. Richard Rothstein, "Taking Aim at Testing," *American School Board Journal*, March 2009, 32.

10. Diane Ravitch, "What Is Campbell's Law?" *Diane Ravitch's Blog* (blog), May 25, 2012, http:// dianeravitch.net/.

11. Eva Baker, et al. "Problems with the Use of Student Test Scores. . . .," 2.

12. Linda Darling-Hammond, "Value-Added Teacher Evaluation: The Hurt Behind the Hype," Commentary, *Education Week*, March 14, 2012, 32.

13. Eva Baker, et al. Problems with the Use of Student Test Scores . . ."

CHAPTER FOUR

1. Jamie Vollmer, "Public School Bashing: A Dangerous Game," American Association of School Administrators, September 2010, www.aasa.org/ content.aspx?id=16438.

2. Richard Rothstein, "How to Fix Our Schools" (issue brief no. 286, Economic Policy Institute, Washington DC, October 14, 2010), 1.

3. Ibid., 4.

4. Barack Obama, quoted in Rothstein, "How to Fix," 1.

5. Arne Duncan, quoted in Richard Rothstein, "The Prospects for No Child Left Behind" (policy memorandum no. 149, Economic Policy Institute, Washington DC, October 13, 2009), 2.

6. Arne Duncan, "An Open letter from Arne Duncan to America's Teachers," *Education Week*, May 2, 2011, 2.

7. Responses to Duncan's letter : www.edweek.org/ew/ articles/2011/05/02/30duncan.h30.html?tkn Pgs. 9–13.

8. Rothstein, "How to Fix."

9. Bill Gates, "Shame Is Not the Answer," Op. Ed., *New York Times*, February 12, 2012.

CHAPTER FIVE

1. Tavis Smiley and Cornel West, *The Rich and the Rest of Us* (New York: Smiley Books, 2012), 117.

2. NACE Salary Survey, 2010–2011. National Association of Colleges and Employers (Bethlehem, Pennsylvania, Volume 50, Issue 1), Winter 2011.

3. Marc S. Tucker, "Standing on the Shoulders of Giants: An Agenda for School Reform" (policy paper, National Center on Education and the Economy, Washington DC, May 24, 2011).

4. Ibid.

5. "Closing the Achievement Gap: Attracting and Retaining Top Third Graduates to Careers in Teaching . . ." McKinsey & Company Report, quoted in Liana Heitin, "U.S. Found to Recruit Fewer Teachers from Top Ranks," *Education Week*, October 20, 2010.

6. Arne Duncan, "An Open Letter from Arne Duncan to America's Teachers," *Education Week,* May 2, 2011, www.edweek.org/ew/articles/2011/05/02/30duncan. h30.html.

7. "Is America Listening to Its Teachers," MetLife Survey of the American Teacher, Executive Summary. (October 17, 2010), 1.

8. Anthony Cody, "Teachers' Letters to Obama: The Sleeping Giant Stirs," *Education Week*, January 20, 2010.

9. Tucker, "Standing on the Shoulders," 12.

10. "Closing the Achievement Gap." McKensie report quoted in Heitin, "U.S. Found."

11. Stephan Sawchuk, "Teachers Pass License Tests at High Rates," *Education Week*, February 1, 2012, 1.

12. Dan Goldhaber, quoted in Sawchuk, "Teachers Pass," 1.

CHAPTER SIX

1. Gary Miron and Leigh Dingerson, "The Charter School Express," *Education Week*, October 1, 2009.

2. Diane Ravitch, "The Myth of Charter Schools," *New York Review of Books*, November 11, 2010, 9.

3. Ibid.

4. Diane Ravitch, quoted in Associated Press, "Charter Schools Expand with Public, Private Money," *Huffington Post*, January 24, 2011, www.huffingtonpost.com/2011/01/21/charter-schools-expand_n_812183.html.

5. *Waiting for "Superman,"* directed by Davis Guggenheim (2010; Hollywood, CA: Paramount Home Entertainment, 2011), DVD.

6. Lesli A. Maxwell, "Accountability Looms Large as Charter Proponents Mull Future," *Education Week*, July 15, 2009.

7. Eileen O'Brien and Chuck Dervarics, "Charter Schools: Finding Out the Facts; At a Glance" Summary Report (Center for Public Education, Alexandria, VA, March 26, 2010), 8.

8. Ibid.

9. Ibid., 16.

10. Margaret Raymond, quoted in Maxwell, "Accountability Looms."

11. Maxwell, "Accountability Looms."

12. "Multiple Choice: Charter School Performance in 16 States" (executive summary, Center for Research on Education Outcomes, Stanford University, Stanford, CA, June 29, 2009), 6.

13. Miron and Dingerson, "The Charter School Express."

CHAPTER SEVEN

1. James Michael Brodie and Frank Wolfe, "The Civil Rights Project, UCLA," *Education Daily*, December 4, 2009, 1.

2. Thomas Hehir, quoted in Sam Dillon, "As U.S. Aid Grows, Oversight Is Urged for Charter Schools," *New York Times,* February 25, 2010, www.nytimes. com?2010/02/25/education/25educ.html?ref =education.

3. Cheryl Karstaedt, quoted in Mark Sherman, "Denver Public Schools Look for Ways to Be More Inclusive," *Education Daily*, December 4, 2009, 3.

4. Ibid.

5. James Michael Brodie, "Report Says Charter Schools Lead to De Facto Segregation," *Education Daily*, February 17, 2010, 2.

6. Mary Ann Zehr, "Evidence Is Limited on Charters' Effect on ELL Achievement," Digital Directions, *Education Week,* March 16, 2009, www.edweek.org/ ew/articles/2009/09/16/03charter.h29.html.

7. Steven F. Wilson, "Success at Scaling in Charter Schools" (working paper, American Enterprise Institute, Washington DC, March 19, 2009), 18.

8. Diane Ravitch, "The Myth of Charter Schools," *New York Review of Books*, November 11, 2010, 7.

9. John Merrow, "When Roads Diverge: Where Will the Charter School Movement Take Education?" Commentary, *Education Week*, December 9, 2009, 26.

10. Ibid.

11. Nirvi Shah, "Academic Gains Vary Widely for Charter Schools," *Education Week*, November 8, 2011.

12. Wilson, "Success at Scaling."

13. Ibid.

14. Jamie Vollmer, *Schools Cannot Do It Alone* (Fairfield, IA: Enlightenment Press, 2010), 21.

CHAPTER EIGHT

1. Grover "Russ" Whitehurst, "Innovation, Motherhood and Apple Pie" (policy brief, Brookings Institution, Washington DC, March 2009), 5.

2. Grover "Russ" Whitehurst, quoted in Claus von Zastrow. "Innovation, Motherhood and Apple Pie: A Conversation with Top Researcher Russ Whitehurst," *Public School Insights* (blog), June 15, 2009, www.learningfirst.org/does-slow-and-steady-win-race-conversation-top-researcher-grover-russ-whitehurst.

3. Whitehurst, "Innovation," 2.

4. Ibid.

5. National Alliance for Public Charter Schools, "Number of Public Charter School Students in U.S. Surpasses Two Million," news release, December 7, 2011, www.publiccharters.org/PressReleasePublic/?id=643.

6. Sarah D. Sparks, "Ed. Blueprint Crystallizes Under State Chiefs' Scrutiny," *Education Daily*, March 24, 2010.

7. National Alliance for Public Charter Schools. Quoted in: "Charter Schools: Finding Out the Facts; Summary Report. At a Glance" (Center for Public Education, Alexandria, VA, March 26, 2010), 4.

8. David Stuit and Thomas Smith, "Teacher Turnover in Charter Schools" (research brief, National Center on School Choice, Vanderbilt University, Nashville, TN, June 2010), 1.

9. Lesli A. Maxwell, "Accountability Looms Large as Charter Proponents Mull Future," *Education Week*, July 15, 2009.

10. Tom Loveless, "How Well Are American Students Learning?" (2009 Brown Center Report on American Education, Brookings Institution, Washington DC, March 2010), 4.

11. Ibid., 30.

12. Gary Miron and Leigh Dingerson, "The Charter School Express," *Education Week*, October 1, 2009, 27.

13. Joe Nathan, quoted in John Merrow, "When Roads Diverge: Where Will the Charter School Movement Take Education?" Commentary, *Education Week*, December 9, 2009, 26.

CHAPTER NINE

1. CREDO Study. Cited in:"Simplistic School Debate Overlooks the Lessons Learned," Today's Debate: Education, *USA Today*, June 22, 2011.

2. Margaret Raymond, quoted in Center for Research on Education Outcomes, "New Stanford Report Finds Serious Quality Challenge in National Charter School Sector," news release, June 15, 2009, 2, http://credo.stanford.edu/reports/National_Release.pdf.

3. Jim Collins, *Good to Great* (New York: HarperCollins, 2001), 165.

4. Ibid.

5. Ibid.

6. Ibid., 178.

7. Ibid.

8. Arne Duncan, quoted in Lesli A. Maxwell, "Accountability Looms Large as Charter Proponents Mull Future," *Education Week*, July 15, 2009.

9. John Merrow, "When Roads Diverge: Where Will the Charter School Movement Take Education?" Commentary, *Education Week*, December 9, 2009, 28.

CHAPTER TEN

1. Programme for International Student Assessment (PISA). Organisation for Economic Co-operation and Development (OECD). Paris, France, 2010.

2. Conversation with Mel Riddle, May 2010.

3. John Gesmonde, "Unions Not Getting Up from Political Knockout Blow," *Connecticut Association of School Administrators (CASA) Newsletter*, May 2010, 4.

4. Mel Riddle, quoted in Gesmonde, "Unions Not Getting Up," 4.

5. Iris Rotberg, quoted in Gerald N. Tirozzi, "The Reality of International Tests," *NewsLeader*, 56, no. 3 (November 2008), 2.

6. Ibid.

7. Ibid.

8. Ibid.

9. Chico Harlan, "Japanese Firm Decrees 'Englishization,' " *Washington Post*, August 7, 2012, 1.

10. Howard Gardner, "Beyond the Herd Mentality: The Minds That We Truly Need in the Future," *Education Week*, September 8, 2012.

11. Ibid.

CHAPTER ELEVEN

1. "How Wall Street Ate the Economy," *BusinessWeek*, June 28, 2008, Cover page headline.

2. Lawrence Mishel and Richard Rothstein, quoted in Gerald N. Tirozzi, "We've Had Enough," *NewsLeader*, 56, no. 2 (October 2008), 2.

3. National Commission on Excellence in Education. *A Nation at Risk: The Imperative for Educational Reform* (Washington DC: U.S. Department of Education, 1983).

4. Andreas Schleicher, quoted in Sean Coughlan, "China: The World's Cleverest Country?" *BBC*

Business News, May 8, 2012, www.bbc.co.uk/news/business-17585201.

5. Coughlan, "China."

6. Andreas Schleicher, quoted in Coughlan, "China."

7. Katherine Boyle, "Debate Rages in Congress, Public over U.S. Olympic Uniforms Made in China," *Washington Post,* July 13, 2012, 2, www.washingtonpost.com/lifestyle/style/debate-rages-in-congress-public-over-us-olympic-uniforms-being-made-in-china/2012/07/13/gJQA74VriW_story.html.

CHAPTER TWELVE

1. Marc S. Tucker, "Standing on the Shoulders of Giants: An Agenda for School Reform" (policy paper, National Center on Education and the Economy, Washington DC, May 24, 2011), 39.

2. Ibid. 12–18.

CHAPTER THIRTEEN

1. Thomas Jefferson, quoted in Gerald N. Tirozzi, "Fighting the Good Fight," *NewsLeader,* 57, no. 2 (September 2009), 2.

2. Alexis de Tocqueville, quoted in David Foster Wallace, *The Pale King,* unfinished novel (New York: New York Times Company, 2011). The author is quoting de Tocqueville in "Democracy in America."

3. Harv Gail L. Sunderman, "The Federal Role in Education: From the Reagan to the Obama

Administration," in "The Evolving Federal Role," Annenberg Institute for School Reform, *Voices in Urban Education* 24 (Summer 2009), 9.

4. Richard Rothstein et al., "Proficiency for All: An Oxymoron" (paper presented at the Symposium Examining America's Commitment to Closing Achievement Gaps: NCLB and Its Alternatives. Campaign for Educational Equity, Teachers College, Columbia University, New York, November 13–14, 2006), 24.

5. Harold Howe II, "Letter to the Commission on Educational Statistics, on the Reauthorization of the National Assessment of Educational Progress (NAEP)," 1988, 1.

6. Daniel Pink, *A Whole New Mind* (New York: Berkley Publishing Group, 2005), 5.

7. John Medina, *Brain Rules* (Seattle: Pear Press, 2008), 69.

8. Howard Gardner, "The Theory of Multiple Intelligence," www.spannj.org/publishers/theory-of -multiple-intellegencies.htm.

9. John Ciardi, quoted in Gerald N. Tirozzi, "No Child Left Behind: In Reading and Math Only?," *NewsLeader*, 53, no. 9 (May 2006), 2.

CHAPTER FOURTEEN

1. Gerald N. Tirozzi, "A Misguided Path to School Improvement," *NewsLeader*, 57, no. 9 (May 2010).

2. Barack Obama, quoted in Tirozzi, "A Misguided Path to School Improvement."

CHAPTER FIFTEEN

1. Gail L. Sunderman, "The Federal Role in Education: From the Reagan to the Obama Administration," in "The Evolving Federal Role," Annenberg Institute for School Reform, *Voices in Urban Education* 24 (Summer 2009), 13.

2. Margaret Spellings, quoted in Brian Stecher, "NCLB Outrages: Susan Ohanian Speaks Out," *Washington Post,* September 13, 2009, www.susanohanian.org/quotes.php

3. Abraham Lincoln, quoted in David Zarensky, "Public Sentiment Is Everything: Lincoln's View of Political Persuasion," *Journal of the Abraham Lincoln Association* 15, no. 2 (1994): 1. This quotation is from Lincoln's first debate with Frederick Douglas, Illinois, 1858.

4. Lester Thurow, quoted in Jamie Vollmer, *Schools Cannot Do It Alone* (Fairfield, IA: Enlightenment Press, 2010), 198.

5. Vollmer, *Schools Cannot,* 198.

6. Peter Drucker, quoted in Vollmer, *Schools Cannot,* 128.

7. John Medina, *Brain Rules* (Seattle: Pear Press, 2008), 275.

8. "Abecedarian Early Intervention Project," *Wikipedia,* last modified July 17, 2012, http://en.wikipedia.org/wiki/Abecedarian_Early_Intervention_Project.

9. Lawrence J. Schweinhart, "Benefits, Costs and Explanation of the High/Scope Perry Pre-School Program" (paper presented at the Meeting of the Society for Research in Child Development, Tampa, FL, April 26, 2003).

10. Betty Hart and Tom R. Risley, *Meaningful Differences* (Baltimore: Brookes, 1995), xix–xxvi.

11. Hubert H. Humphrey, "Quotation Details: Quotation #29565 from Classic Quotes," *The Quotations Page,* accessed October 24, 2012, www .quotationspage.com/quote/29565.html.

12. Rand Corporation, "Investment in Summer Learning Programs Can Help Stop the 'Summer Slide,'" news release, June 13, 2011, www.rand.org/news/ press/2011/06/13.html.

13. Nancy Devine, quoted in Rand Corporation, "Investment."

14. Medina, *Brain Rules*, 100.

CONCLUSION

1. Ken Kesey, quoted in Jim Collins, *Good to Great* (New York: HarperCollins, 2001), 41. This quotation originally appeared in Tom Wolfe's *The Electric Kool-Aid Acid Test*.

INDEX

A

Accountability: seeking, for student achievement and fiscal responsibility, 124–125; systems of, 65–67
"Accountability madness," 177
Achievement gap, 15, 24
ACT, 49, 138
ADHD, 111
Advanced placement, 49, 138, 204
Alternate certification, 15–36; and original mission of Teach for America (TFA), 22–25; for principals, 28–36; and programs like Teach for America: do they help low-performing students?, 26–28; and Teach for America: has it helped our schools?, 18–22
American Association of School Administrators, 167
American Federation of Teachers, 76, 91
American Indian reservations, 115–116
Assessment, teacher. *See* Evaluation, teacher
Attendance, student, 204
Attrition, 107–111

B

BBC Business News Periodical, 153
Beeley, Angela, 14
Berry, Barnett, 28
Bill and Melinda Gates Foundation, 24–25
Black Panther trials, 222
Blame avoidance, 135
Bloomberg, Michael, 41–42
"Blueberry Story," 111
Boston, Massachusetts, 104
Brain Research, 208–209
Brain Rules (Medina), 179, 208, 227–228
Breakthrough Schools (BTSs), 212
Broad Foundation, 24–25

Brown Center Report on American Education, 117–118

BTSs. *See* Breakthrough Schools (BTSs)

Bush (George W.) administration, 40, 94, 113, 169

Bush, George W., 172, 173

C

Campbell, Donald, 45

Campbell's Law, 45

Canada, 139

Canada, Geoffrey, 107–108

Career ladders, for teachers, 73–75

Center for Education Reform, 102

Center for Research on Education Outcomes (CREDO), 98–102, 123, 124, 126

Center for Teaching Quality, 28

Central Falls, Rhode Island, 188

Charter management organizations (CMOs), 116

"Charter School Express" *(Education Week)*, 93, 119

Charter schools: closing low-performing, 126; as dream denied, 91–96; and equity problem, 103–120; getting, back on track, 121–130; as innovative and effective, 113–120; performance of, 96–102; as primary area of school reform, 232; slowing down rapid expansion of, 127–130; using, as incubators, 122; using evaluation data responsibly with, 123–124

Chicago Public Schools, 41–43; Teacher Advancement Program, 41

Children Zone (Harlem), 108

China, 139, 152–154

"China: The World's Cleverest Country?" *(BBC Business News Periodical)*, 153

Chinese language, 146

Ciardi, John, 180

Civic engagement, in school reform improvement initiatives, 200–202

Civil Rights Project (University of California, Los Angeles), 103–104

Closure issue, 118–119

Cody, Anthony, 76–77

Coleman Report, 52

College acceptance, 204

Collins, Jim, xiii, 127–130

Columbia University Teachers College, 26

Comer, James, 223

Comer model, 223–224

Comer School Development Program, 223

Commission on the Skills of the American Workforce, 150

Community education, 53, 219–225, 230

"Compulsory, definition of," 139–140

Connecticut, 3, 64, 69–70, 197, 198

Conte Community School (New Haven, Connecticut), 220–223

Cuomo, Andrew, 94–95

D

Darling-Hammond, Linda, 19, 46–47

Data: in disaggregated format, 204; evaluation, 123–124

Deming, W. Edward, 38–40

Democrats for Education Reform, 24–25, 94–95

Denver Public Schools, 104, 105

Dervarics, Chuck, 99, 100

Devine, Nancy, 227

Dingerson, Leigh, 93, 102, 119

Disabilities, students with, 48, 138; underrepresentation of, 104–106

Disabilities Act (1978), 170–171

Domenich, Dan, 167

Doris and Donald Fisher Fund, 25

Drucker, Peter, 206

Duncan, Arne, 37, 41–43, 53–56, 61, 75, 76, 98, 101, 117, 129, 186, 192

E

Early childhood education, 213–219

Ebbinghaus, Hermann, 228

Economic Policy Institute (EPI), 38–39, 44, 46, 50, 174

ED. See U.S. Department of Education (ED)

Edison Schools of California, 25

Education Commission of the States, 28

Education crisis, 149

Education Enhancement Act (EEA), 64, 69, 198, 199

Education Summit (NBC), 96

Education Week, 38, 55, 93

Educational connoisseurs, 33, 66

EEA. See Education Enhancement Act (EEA)

Eisenhower administration, 144

Elementary and Secondary Education Act (1965), 170–171

ELLs. See English Language Learners

"English Firm Decrees 'Englishization'" (Washington Post), 145

English language, 145–146

English language learners (ELLs), 9, 19, 31, 47, 66, 96, 125, 227; under enrollment of, 106–107

Equity problem, 103–120; and racial isolation, 103–104; and

under enrollment of English language learners, 106–107; and underrepresentation of students with disabilities, 104–106. *See also under* Charter Schools

Evaluation, teacher, 65–67; certification, 71–73; criteria for, 66; use of peer evaluators for, 67–68

Evaluation data, responsible use of, 123–124

Expulsion rates, 204

F

Faculty, replacing, 188–191

Federal government, role of: getting, back on track, 195–230; and holding states and school districts accountable for student achievement (recommendation 4), 202–206; as primary area of school reform, 232–233; and promoting community education (recommendation 7), 219–225; and promoting expanded summer school programs (recommendation 8), 226–229; and promoting preschool and early childhood education (recommendation 6), 213–219; and providing leadership in education research (recommendation 5),

206–213; and providing research-based federal recommendations to inform state-based school (recommendation 1), 196–199; and reauthorizing and reforming NCLB now (recommendation 2), 199

Federal school reform initiatives: and getting federal role back on track, 195–230; and is proficiency for all students possible or desirable?, 173–176; and what happened to local control?, 165–181

Finland, 133, 139, 140, 159

Finn-Stevenson, Matia, 218

Fisher, Donald, 25

Flint, Michigan, 223

Flom, Jason, 55

Florida, alternate certification in, 30–31

Fordham University, 21

Foundation leaders, 15, 52, 77, 133–134

Foundations, 94–95

Funding, 166

G

Gap stores, 25

Gardner, Howard, 146–147, 179

Gates, Bill, 57

George Washington University, 141

Germany, 153

Gesmonde, John, 3
Good Morning America (television show), 96
Good to Great (Collins), xiii, 127
"Great Conversation," 201
Guggenheim, Davis, 97, 98, 107–108
Guthrie, James, 40

H

Haimson, Leonie, 55–56
Harlem Children Zone, 108
Harvard University, 104, 146
Head Start, 214–218
Hedge funds, 94–95
Hehir, Thomas, 104
High-performing schools, identification of, 211–212
High/Scope Educational Research Foundation, 215
"Honest Recruitment Tool," 5–11
Hong Kong, China, 139, 153–154
Houston Independent School District (Texas), 172
"How Wall Street Ate the Economy" *(Business Week)*, 150
Howe, Harold, II, 174–175
Hoxby, Caroline, 108–109
Humphrey, Hubert, 217

I

IDEA. *See* Individuals with Disabilities Education Act (IDEA)

Improving America's Schools Act (1994), 170–171
India, 152
Individuals with Disabilities Education Act (IDEA), 48, 195–196
Indonesia, 152
Innovation: concerns regarding, 115–116; and effectiveness, 113–120
Institute of Education Sciences, 207
International Baccalaureate examinations, 49, 138, 204
International comparisons: and allowing for teacher and principal international exchanges (recommendation 5), 160; analyzing factors that influence (recommendation 3), 158–159; assessing results of, in more positive way (recommendation 2), 158; and continuing to develop online capabilities (recommendation 7), 158–159; and convening international conference of educators (recommendation 6), 160; and determining why U.S. reform strategies are foreign to other countries, 159; getting, back on track, 157–161; and new look at Programme for International

Student Assessment (PISA), 133–147; as primary area of school reform, 232; understanding and respecting complex realities of (recommendation 1), 157–158

International job market, 152–155

International rankings. *See* Programme for International Student Assessment (PISA)

J

Jackson, Michael, 3

Japan, 151–153; and false economic expectations based on student test scores, 145–147

Jefferson, Thomas, 166

Johns Hopkins University, 189

Johnson Administration, 214

Juneau, Denise, 115–116

K

Kantor, Harvey, 171–172

Karstaedt, Cheryl, 104, 105

Kennedy, Edward, 169

Kesey, Ken, 231

Klein, Joel, 41–42

Knowledge Alliance, 114

Knowledge Is Power Program, 110

Kopp, Wendy, 18

Korea, 139

L

"Lake Woebegone" effect, 169, 176

Leadership, in education research, 206–213

Levine, Arthur, 26

Lincoln, Abraham, 200

Los Angeles, California, 104

Lottery, 97

Loveless, Tom, 118

Lowe, Robert, 171–172

Low-performing students, 26–28

M

"Mad as Hell" *(Education Week)*, 14

Massachusetts, 106; alternate certification in, 30

Massachusetts Institute of Technology, 201

Mathematica Policy Research, 42

Mathematics, 208

Mathis, William, 43

McKinsey & Company, 63

Medina, John, 179, 208, 227–228

Mentor teacher, 86

Merrow, John, 108, 109, 130

MetLife Survey of the American Teacher, 76

Metropolitan Nashville Public Schools (Tennessee), 42

Mexico, 152, 153

Michigan, 215

Michigan State University, 223

Miner, Barbara, 21–24, 27

Minnesota, 92

Miron, Gary, 93, 102, 119

Mishel, Lawrence, 150

Misplaced blame, history of, 150–152

Montana, 115–116

"Myth of Charter Schools" *(New York Review of Books)*, 93

N

NAEP. *See* National Assessment of Educational Progress (NAEP)

Naison, Mark, 21

NAPCS. *See* National Alliance for Public Charter Schools (NAPCS)

NASSP. *See* National Association of Secondary School Principals (NASSP)

Nathan, Joe, 119–120

Nation at Risk: The Imperative for Educational Reform (National Commission on Excellence in Education), 150–152, 197–199

National Alliance for Public Charter Schools (NAPCS), 99, 100, 117

National Assessment of Educational Progress (NAEP), 99, 172–173, 203–204

National Association of Secondary School Principals (NASSP), 139, 212

National Board Certified Teachers, 76, 210

National Board for Professional Teaching Standards, 210

National Center on Education and the Economy, 62

National Center on Performance Incentives, 40, 41

National Center on School Choice, 117

National Charter School Research Project, 116

National Common Core Standards, 204

National Education Association, 76

National Public Radio (NPR), 96

"National report card," 204–205

NBC, 96

NCLB. *See* No Child Left Behind (NCLB)

New Hampshire, alternate certification in, 29–30

New Haven, Connecticut, 221, 222

New Mexico, 191

New York City, 108; performance bonus plan, 41–42; public schools, 19, 41

New York Review of Books, 93

New York Times, 94

New Zealand, 139

No Child Left Behind (NCLB), 75, 101, 186, 197, 199, 203;

as law of land, 168–170; origination of, 172–173; reauthorization and reform of, 199; testing problem in, 177–181; as unprecedented shift in federal role, 170–172

NPR. *See* National Public Radio (NPR)

O

Obama, Barak, 37, 53, 75–76, 98, 188

Obama administration, 61, 76–78, 91, 94, 98, 118, 133–134, 149, 150, 186, 188–193, 200–203, 205, 206, 214–216, 218, 219, 224–230

O'Brien, Eileen, 99, 100

Office of Special Education Programs (U.S. Department of Education), 104

Olympic Games (2012; England), 154–155

Online capabilities, 161

Oprah (television show), 96

Organization for Economic Co-operation and Development, 135

P

Paige, Rod, 169, 172

Pay-for-performance (PFP), 32; final warning about, 49–50; and performance pay as hallmark of business

community (myth 1), 38–40; and research supports pay for performance for teachers (myth 2), 40–43_; separating myth from reality in, 37–50; and standardized test scores represent an equitable and responsible way to evaluate teacher performance (myth 4), 45–49; and teachers will be positively motivated by added financial incentives provided by, initiatives (myth 3), 44–45

PBS NewsHour, 108

Peabody College, Vanderbilt University, 40

Peer evaluation, to support teacher evaluation, 68–70

PFP. *See* Pay-for-performance (PFP)

Pink, Daniel, 177

PISA. *See* Programme for International Student Assessment (PISA)

Policy gurus, xiii–xiv, 12, 15, 77, 179, 203

Preschool and early childhood education, 213–219

Princeton University, 18

"Principal pretenders," 31–32

Principals: evaluation assistance for, 72–73; indicators of quality in, 204; international exchange among, 160; role of, as instructional leaders, 67–68

Privatization, 24, 25, 93, 95–96

Proficiency for all, as oxymoron, 174

Programme for International Student Assessment (PISA), 133–147, 153, 158, 160; and contextual questions regarding international rankings, 137–138; description of, 135–136; and international rankings of student achievement as predictors of economic growth, 143–144; and Japan story, 144–147; new look at, 136–138; and role of poverty, 140–143; and Russia story, 144; and where U.S. really stands, 138–140

Pruett, G. K., 55

PSATs, 49

Public Education Network, 24

Puriefoy, Wendy, 24

R

Race to the Top, 4, 54, 60, 61, 64, 98, 101, 105, 168, 183–184, 199, 203, 213, 219, 228–229

Racial isolation, 103–104

Rand Corporation, 41, 227

"Ratings game," 139–140

Ravitch, Diane, 34, 93–95, 107, 108

Raymond, Margaret, 101, 126

Reading, 207

Reagan administration, 197

Rich and the Rest of Us, The (Smiley and West), 61

Riddle, Mel, 139–141

Rotberg, Iris, 141–142

Rothstein, Richard, 44, 46, 52, 150, 174

RTT. *See* Race to the Top

Rush to judgment mentality, 136

Russia, 151–153

Russia story, 144

S

Salary ranges, teacher, 204

San Diego, California, 104

San Francisco, California, 25

SATs, 49, 138

Schleicher, Andreas, 153, 154

School completion rates, 204

School Improvement Grants (SIG), 4, 32, 60, 64, 98, 168, 199, 203, 219, 228–229; four models of, 185; and helping schools or holding them hostage, 185–187; and what does it really take to turn school around?, 187–188; and what does it take to replace staff and faculty?, 188–191; and what happens when SIG money goes away?, 191–193

School of the 21st Century (21C) model (Yale University), 218

School violence, incidences of, 204

Schools Cannot Do It Alone (Vollmer), 201

Schools without Diversity: Education Management Organizations, Charter Schools and the Demographic Stratification of the American School System (Brodie), 106

Schuerman, Patrick, 40

Science, 208

Shaming, 57

Shanghai, China, 139, 153–154

Shanker, Albert, 91–95

SIG. *See* School Improvement Grants (SIG) initiatives

Singapore, 139, 159

Smiley, Tavis, 61

Soviet Union, 44, 144

Spellings, Margaret, 199

Springfield, Missouri, 218

Sputnik 1, 144

Staff, replacing, 188–191

Standardized testing, 45–49

Stanford University, 19, 23, 98–99

"State report card," 204

Student attendance, 204

Summer school programs, expanding, 226–229

Sunderman, Carl, 197

Suspension rates, 204

T

Teach for America (TFA): faithfulness to original mission of, 22–25; as helping America's schools, 17–22; and low-performing students, 26–28

Teacher Advancement Program (TAP; Chicago), 42, 43

Teacher bashing, 12–13; rationale for, 51–58; and state and district policies regarding shaming and blaming, 56–58; and support of national leaders for teachers, 54–56

Teacher preparation programs, reforming, 78–86

Teacher reform: and conducting White House conference on "Listening to the Voices of Teachers," 75–78; cost of, 60–62; and dramatically increasing teacher salaries (recommendation 1), 62–65; and establishing teacher evaluation certificates (recommendation 5), 71–73; and focusing teacher evaluation and systems of accountability on skill sets and classroom outcomes (recommendation 2), 65–67; and improving teacher induction into profession and on-the-job training (recommendation 9), 86–87; and providing career ladders for teachers (recommendation 6), 73–75; recommendations for, 59–88; and reforming teacher preparation programs (recommendation 8), 78–86; and strengthening role of principals as instructional leaders (recommendation 3), 67–68; and using peer evaluators to support teacher evaluation (recommendation 4), 68–70

Teachers: career ladders for, 73–75; as center of education universe, 87–88; improving induction of, into profession, 86–87; indicators of quality in, 204; international exchange among, 160; and lament of Angela Beeley, 14; personal reflection on new realities for, 5–11

Teachers College, Columbia University, 26

Teaching: best practices in, 209–210; disincentives in choice of, as career, 5–11; interns, 18–19; as primary area of school reform, 231–232

Tennessee, 41

Tenth Amendment (U.S. Constitution), 165, 167

Tenure decisions, 86–87

"Texas miracle," 172

TFA. See Teach for America (TFA)

Thurow, Lester, 201

Title I, 195–196, 228–229

Tocqueville, Alexis de, 168

TPSs, 121–125. See Traditional public schools (TPSs)

Traditional public schools (TPSs), 91–92, 98–102, 105–106, 121–125

Tucker, Marc, 62–63, 159

Turnaround schools, 15, 191

Twain, Mark, 136

21st Century Community Learning Centers, 219

U

Universal proficiency, fallacy of, 174, 175

University of California, Los Angeles, 103–104

University of North Carolina, 215

U.S. Census Bureau, 139

U.S. Congress, 149, 154, 168, 201, 202

U.S. Constitution, 165, 202–203

U.S. Department of Education (ED), 43, 105, 167, 184–186, 201–203, 206, 209, 210;

Office of Special Education Programs, 104

Utah, alternate certification in, 28–29

V

Van Houten, Mrs., 55

Vanderbilt University, 40–42

Visiting Nurse Association, 220

Vollmer, Jamie, 51, 111–112, 201

W

Waiting for Superman (documentary film), 96, 97, 107

Walker, Scott, 14

Wallace Family Foundation, 25, 227

Wal-Mart, 25

Walton, Sam, 25

Washington Post, 27, 145, 154

Weaver, Barbara, 75

Welner, Kevin, 43

West, Cornel, 61

Western Michigan University, 93

What Works Clearinghouse, 207

Whitehurst, Russ, 113, 114

Whole New Mind (Pink), 177

Wilson, Steven, 107, 110–111

Wisconsin, 14

Wood, George, 24–25

Y

Yale University, 218, 223

Z

Zigler, Edward, 218